D1596742

Stories in Your
HANDS

Discover Your Authentic Destiny
Using Palmistry & Tarot

CYNTHIA CLARK

Illustrations from the Rider-Waite Tarot Deck® reproduced by permission of U.S. Games Systems, Inc., Stamford, CT 06902 USA. Copyright ©1971 by U.S. Games Systems, Inc. Further reproduction prohibited. The Rider-Waite Tarot Deck® is a registered trademark of U.S. Games Systems, Inc.

Archway Publishing books may be ordered through booksellers or by contacting:

Archway Publishing
1663 Liberty Drive
Bloomington, IN 47403
www.archwaypublishing.com
1 (888) 242-5904

Because of the dynamic nature of the Internet, any web addresses or links contained in this book may have changed since publication and may no longer be valid. The views expressed in this work are solely those of the author and do not necessarily reflect the views of the publisher, and the publisher hereby disclaims any responsibility for them.

Any people depicted in stock imagery provided by Thinkstock are models, and such images are being used for illustrative purposes only. Certain stock imagery © Thinkstock.

ISBN: 978-1-4808-4018-8 (sc)
ISBN: 978-1-4808-4017-1 (hc)
ISBN: 978-1-4808-4019-5 (e)

Library of Congress Control Number: 2017900043

Print information available on the last page.

Archway Publishing rev. date: 01/20/2017

Contents

Dedication

For my clients, thank you for allowing me to live my
authentic destiny by helping you connect with yours.

Acknowledgements

WITHOUT THE ASSISTANCE OF A GREAT MANY people, this book would not have happened. I would like to personally thank my parents, Wes and Louise Warner, who have always supported me and my work. Thanks to my two brothers Ken and Wendel. Thanks to my editor, Karen Connington. Thanks to Cheryl Murphy, Ellie Scott and Gabrielle Andreozetti for reading my original manuscript and giving me great feedback. Thanks to my friends Andrea Rasband, Trina Jones, Angela Rose, Susanna Rose, Kathy Darrow, Carlin Brightwell, Jay Shumaker, Camille Lione, Pat Newkam and Pamela Stevens-Steffensen for believing in me. Special thanks to David Card, Jimmy and Carlene Carlson, Bill and Suzanne Jun and Shae Singer for giving me a chance to share and develop my work. Thank you Kyle Piorkowski for your audio assistance. Thanks to Emily and Virginia Hornblower for your fresh insights and feedback. Thank you John Hornblower and Catherine Fishman for your helpful wordsmithing. Thank you Mike Kulik for technical assistance. Thank you Jim Williams for everything. Thanks to all my clients and readers for taking this journey with me toward greater understanding of our souls and our authentic destinies.

Foreword

THREE YEARS AGO I EXPERIENCED A CAREER CRI-
sis. For the previous twenty-seven years, I had earned a generous living trading convertible bonds and derivatives with in-
stitutional investors. Then in a relatively short period of time,
about eighteen months, my earnings power evaporated. Rapid
advances in information technology, vast increases in regula-
tion, and adverse market forces such as unprecedentedly low
interest rates and low business confidence stemming from what
I would describe as an anti-business, anti-Wall Street political
climate together provided the perfect storm to wipe away a long
and healthy career.

Then I met Cynthia Clark. Cynthia read my hands and
helped me discover talents and personal strengths that I had either taken for granted or didn't even know that I had. "A healer
of healers," Cynthia told me was my strongest and most unique
trait. "The Sun and the Moon" were my dominant psychologi-
cal archetypes. Under Cynthia's guidance and over a period of
about nine months, I found the courage and wisdom to reinvent
myself as a small business broker, a mergers and acquisitions
advisor. I founded a new company, www.vraspen.com, and am
now thriving with more business than I can handle.

I honestly doubt that I could have managed this career tran-
sition without Cynthia's deep personal insights and guidance.
Cynthia has an amazing talent. I'm sure she will be famous one

day. I urge you to read her book to gain insights for yourself, to unlock your hidden potential, and as Cynthia would put it, to reach your Authentic Destiny.

Sincerely,
John G. Hornblower, CFA
Aspen, CO

Introduction

INSIDE ALL OF US ARE STORIES. THESE STORIES include our personality, our soul's longing, our hopes and dreams, our mental and emotional expressiveness, and how our own personal reality is playing out. What are your stories? What stories would you still like to tell? Your palms hold the road map to these stories and to the rest of your life. You can think of your hands as extensions of your brain. The brain is more closely connected with the hands than with any other part of the body. Neuroscientists have confirmed that the lines in the hands mimic the neural pathways in the brain and that these lines change over time, a principle in alignment with the study of epigenetics. According to Dr. Bruce Lipton, author of *The Biology of Belief,* genes and DNA do not control our biology. Instead, DNA is controlled by signals from outside the cell. These signals include messages from our positive and negative thoughts and emotions.

The study of palmistry, also known as chirology, is thousands of years old. The lines are the most complicated and changeable aspect of palmistry. The pictures below show the same hand over a three-year time lapse. The picture on the left was taken in 2009, the right in 2012. See how many differences you can spot.

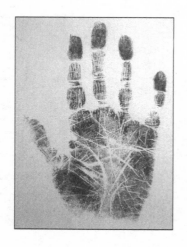 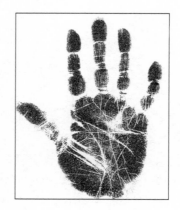

Even if you don't know anything about palmistry, a close inspection of these two photos reveals how much the hands can actually change over time. I would describe the picture on the left as "stressed out." There are lines moving in every direction and several stress or challenge lines running from this woman's thumb ball region across the hand diagonally. If you look at the second picture, you will notice that the lines overall are reduced and not as thick. Her thumb is quite weak in the first picture compared to the second picture, representing an increase in her willpower over time and her ability to make changes according to her desires. Her middle finger is straighter in the second picture. Any time a finger bends it indicates stress, and in the middle finger relates to worrying about making decisions. Horizontal lines in the fingers represent blockages and stress. You can see quite a few of these in the left picture and fewer in the right. Each section of finger actually represents a different area in your life, so analysis can become quite technical and specific depending on where a horizontal line shows up. We won't explore the details in depth here, but just know that horizontal lines in the fingers display stress and vertical lines display flow. It is common for people to have both types of lines in their fingers. Here is the comparison again, this time with markings highlighted in the first picture.

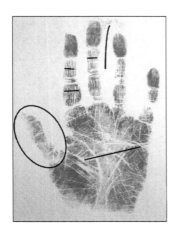 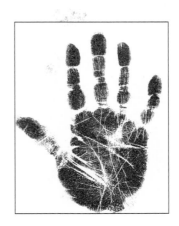

Now we have an idea how the lines and fingers change over time based on our decisions and how we interact with our environment. How you think and feel, and even the chakras or energy centers in your body, reflect through your palm. By understanding how your "map" is reading, you can work with the information to make positive changes in your life in all areas: physically, emotionally, mentally and spiritually. Over time, your hands will reflect these changes. We've seen the possibilities in the hands of this woman, who transformed her life, reduced her stress, and aligned herself more deeply with her authentic self.

Other studies have been done with meditation and the brain. The work of Dr. Joe Dispenza, author of *You Are the Placebo*, proves that you can change your reality by changing your thoughts and emotions. Doctors in Japan and Korea are even testing the impacts of surgery on the lines in the hand in altering the future realities of their patients. Just imagine the possibilities of living a healthier, happier life if you understood the imbalances marked in your own hands and knew how to change them.

There are three branches to palmistry. Chirognomy (pronounced keer-og-no-mee) relates to the study of the fingers, palm and thumb and how they relate to each other. For the purposes of this book, I will be guiding you in chirognomy and line type identification. There is also the study of fingerprints and palmar prints, known as dermatoglyphics, "derma" meaning skin and "glyphics" meaning markings. These represent the permanent and unchangeable aspect of your soul, your soul imprint. Finally, chiromancy relates to interpreting line formations, partly for predicting the future. By understanding the meaning behind the hands, we learn to recognize aspects of ourselves and how they reflect in our fingers and palms. This knowledge empowers us, allowing us to write our own stories and watch how they impact our future. Isn't it time we moved past the old, untrue dogma that says "your hands tell you when you're going to die?" It's time that palmistry reclaims its place in history as the esteemed art and science it once was. During the Renaissance, palmistry was taught in universities throughout Italy. In fact, palmistry is so useful, specific and helpful, I have completely altered my life to share it with you.

The Archetypes and the Tarot

The concept of archetypes became popular with the Swiss psychotherapist, Carl Jung, who believed that we inherited certain traits from a collective unconscious. As these imprints become conscious, the idea is that we act out and exhibit them through our personality, or archetype. The tarot (pronounced tare-oh) has been around since at least the fifteenth Century. It is currently the most popular divination tool in the world, consisting of seventy-eight cards divided into two sections, the Major Arcana, meaning "big secrets" and the Minor Arcana, meaning "little secrets." Each of the cards depicts a picture that represents deeper truths layered in symbolism and meaning. The concept behind the tarot is that by asking questions to the cards, your higher self will attract the answer energetically as you draw forth each card in response to your question. If you are skeptical about this, I simply urge you to use them for a period of time and discover for yourself the accuracy of this tool. The Major Arcana, consisting of twenty-two cards, represent the journey of life, or the archetypal influences that affect all of us. They were created to symbolically express particular traits of the psyche and all of them have positive aspects, even ones with "scary" titles such as Death or the Fool. In this text, I will be using a single gender for each individual archetype, based on the picture of the tarot card. Of course, you may be male or female and embody any of the archetypes. I will also be using the English spelling of the word "judgement" since this is how it is written on the card.

Connecting Palmistry with the Tarot

As a student of metaphysical studies for many years and as someone who likes to connect viewpoints and ideas, I've made a new discovery. I've discovered that the hands reflect the archetypes of the tarot and the Major Arcana. These archetypes have appeared in every single set of over 6,000 pairs of hands I've examined in my career so far. Are you a Magician, an Emperor, or the World? Join me on a journey of discovery and exploration. By knowing and understanding what the hands are expressing, and identifying our primary archetypes, we can access more clarity and mindfulness around specific themes we are working to master and demonstrate. This in turn helps us to be more joyful and fulfilled, by connecting us to our authentic selves, our true purpose and our full potential. When you know and connect deeply to your archetype, you can understand and balance your life from a whole new perspective. In other words, you don't have to make yourself "wrong" anymore. You can embrace your authentic self and celebrate the aspects that make you "you." Because you should be a celebration! You are a unique Being of Light who holds keys to living a life that only you can fulfill. It is my hope and desire that as you discover deeper truths about yourself, you will be inspired to take action to grow and evolve in your own consciousness. You deserve to live in total alignment with your authentic destiny and the world deserves to receive what only you can deliver.

Structure of This Book

I am excited to share this valuable information with you and hope this book will become a valuable reference for you to use over and over again. This book focuses on the Major Arcana, which I've divided into the text by chapter. The first chapter I've labeled "Chapter 0" to stay in alignment with each card's corresponding number. The first card of the tarot deck is the Fool, which is traditionally numbered as zero, or "ground zero" in the journey of the soul's evolution through the cards of the tarot deck. The pictures of the cards are from the Rider-Waite tarot deck, the most popular of all decks (used by permission). There are hundreds of other decks out there as well and I encourage you to get a deck that resonates with you.

In the following chapters, you will learn more about each of the archetypes and how to identify them in your own hand. It's important to know that we can learn and grow from all of the archetypes, but identifying your own is key to navigating your soul's pathway and evolution. Everyone will have at least one archetype, while others will have as many as three.

Each chapter includes instructions for you to work with the archetypes in positive and productive ways. Through reading this book, you will be able to:

1. **Identify the physical, mental, emotional and spiritual attributes of each archetype.** This will allow you to recognize the attributes in yourself and

others, and open to the archetype yourself by aligning with the description.

2. **Quickly identify key words associated with each archetype.** This will assist you in learning the themes of each archetype easily.

3. **Identify the type of hand associated with each archetype.** You will be able to identify your own archetypes this way.

4. **Learn how to balance the energies within each archetype and restore alignment with your authentic self, using mudras, questions for growth and truth statements.** A mudra is the act of placing your hands in a specific position in order to connect with the energy of a specific archetype. Mudras have been practiced in yoga for thousands of years as a form of mind/body connection. Since the hands reflect the personality, various mudras can help you to engage with certain aspects of that personality.

To do a quick balance, I recommend placing your hands in a mudra position. Inhale and exhale deeply for a few breaths. Invoke the archetype by saying, "I call in and welcome the healing energy of the Fool (or the energy of whichever archetype you like) to balance my body, mind and spirit." Think about breathing in the positive energy of the archetype as you inhale. As you exhale, breathe out any imbalances. Close your eyes as you hold this position. Then, open your eyes and read through the truth statements out loud while still holding the mudra. For a longer balance, read through each of the growth questions one at a time, close your eyes and meditate on the question. Allow sufficient time for an answer to come through. Keep a special archetype journal next to you so that you can write down any ideas that come forward. This is a great way to receive guidance from your higher self and open the positive aspects of each archetype. You may also order recorded meditations for each archetype through www.storiesinyourhands.com.

5. **Identify which chakra or chakras are associated with each archetype.** Chakras are the energy centers in your body, beginning near your perineum and continuing to the top of your head.

There are seven commonly recognized chakras that impact your well-being on many levels. The seven chakras are the root, sacral, solar plexus, heart, throat, third eye and crown. The term "chakra" is a Sanskrit word meaning "wheel." These energy centers spin in your body and radiate certain color spectrums of light. When a chakra is out of balance, you will experience various forms of illness or emotional distress. Each of the archetypes is associated with one or more chakras. I recommend doing the balancing steps I just mentioned in a standing position for all the archetypes relating to the lower chakras – the root, sacral or solar plexus. Otherwise, you may prefer to sit, either on the floor or in a chair. The process of standing simply helps ground your energy.

6. **Identify how each archetype may be out of balance.** Imbalances may appear as too much or too little energy within the archetype. These imbalances show up through actions, emotions and chakras.

7. **Relate the characteristics of each archetype to your home life, your work and your relationships.**
8. **Identify the best compatibilities within each archetype.** Learn which archetypes naturally get along with other.
9. **Identify challenging compatibilities within each archetype.** Learn which archetypes don't connect easily to each other.
10. **Identify the opposite archetype.** I recommend balancing for the opposite archetype, especially if you have an imbalance that is severe.
11. **Discover how the hands of famous people reflect specific archetypes.** Throughout this book, I will be looking at the archetypes of some famous people, both real and fictional. For the real people, I categorized them based on their hands and not their personalities. I found many of the hand photos online at a site called handresearch.com. I also researched specific people online and sorted through dozens of photos. Over the years, I have paid attention during movies when someone held up their hand. I would actually pause the movie and take a picture of the television screen in order to analyze the hand later. By the way, I am always interested in famous hand prints. Please send them my way if you happen to have any yourself! If you do not see the famous person listed as expressing a certain archetype, I suggest looking at the imbalances, for not everyone displays their archetype in public. The archetypes provide deeper insights into public figures, beyond the spotlight of the media. Some people may be listed more than once throughout this book, since they express more than one archetype. I've identified archetypes for fictional characters based on their character traits.

Identifying Archetypes in the Hand

You will be reading your own hands throughout this book, and hopefully your friends' and family's hands too. To do that, let's focus on the very basics of palmistry by looking at four specific features in the hands: finger length, palm shape, strong finger(s) (which may differ from left and right hand) and "type" of lines. While this may seem like a small number of things to examine, do not underestimate their usefulness. These archetypal influences affect your life in powerful ways and over time. As a baby you haven't formed your permanent hand structure until you are about five or six years old. This is when the personality truly emerges and solidifies in the person. This is also when the brain waves move into a more adult frequency pattern. As a young child, your brain stays in the lower frequencies of theta and delta, also known as the sleeping brain states. In other words, you are completely in your subconscious until about the age of six. This is also when the hand shape archetypes emerge. After this time, the brain frequency moves into the alpha and beta states, also known as the conscious states. Yes, of course there are many more details to learn from hand reading, including soul agenda, potentials, environmental impact and personal developments, and I encourage a full analysis to discover the complete picture. It is my opinion that the archetypes interact and influence all the features in the hand, providing a platform of knowledge to benefit from.

We'll begin with a diagram of the hand. The fingers are all named after the Roman gods and palmists refer to them by that god's name. Jupiter is the index finger. Saturn is the middle finger. Apollo is the ring finger and Mercury is the little finger. A phalange refers to a section of a finger, or to one of the three ascending parts of each finger. The percussion refers to the edge of the palm under the little finger side. The major lines are the heart line, head line, fate line and life line. They are called major lines because they are on every person's hand in some variation, with the occasional exception to the fate line. The rascettes are the lines that encircle the wrist. There are usually three or four of these present at the base of the palm. The thumb represents willpower and has a line present at the edge of the palm separating it visually from the palm. Keep in mind that lines vary tremendously from person to person and your major lines may not always resemble the diagrams.

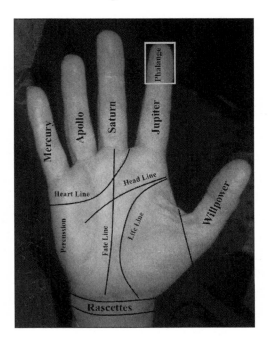

First, you will be identifying an element through finger length and palm shape. The four sacred elements are earth, fire, water and air. They have been described as the matter of our universe. These elements have been studied since ancient times as ways to connect with ourselves and the world we all live in. They were identified in ancient Babylonia, Egypt, China, India, Japan and Greece, where Plato was the first person known to use the term "element." This ancient wisdom is still applicable today.

Each person has a primary element in the hands that corresponds with earth, fire, water or air. Your primary element is located in your hand shape. Children under the age of four most likely have Earth as their primary element, since this element corresponds with the physical world and they are busy absorbing everything in it, like a sponge. They are learning how to function in a new environment and need Earth to do it effectively. The type of lines you have in your palm determine your secondary element. Knowing your primary and secondary elements helps to give you insight into your personality profile and archetype(s). What primary element are you? Let's take a look.

Determine Your Primary Element

Fingers can be either long or short and the palm can be either square or rectangular. No configuration is better or worse than another.

Measurement 1: Compare the length of your middle finger, also known as Saturn, with the length of the palm. If this finger is LESS than three-fourths the palm length, then you have short fingers. If this finger is three-fourths the length of the palm or longer, then you have long fingers. If you are right on the edge of this measurement, pull the hand back and look at it. Do your fingers seem long or short to you? Go with that instinct.

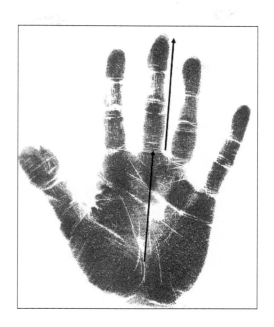

Measurement 2: Compare the length of the palm versus the width. Take the measurement from the base of the Saturn finger vertically to the rascettes. Then compare that length with the width of the palm from the middle of the percussion to the base of the thumb. If the two measurements are within one centimeter of each other, then you have a square palm. If the length is more than one centimeter longer, then you have a long, rectangular palm. If you're on the cusp, pull the hand back and go with your intuition.

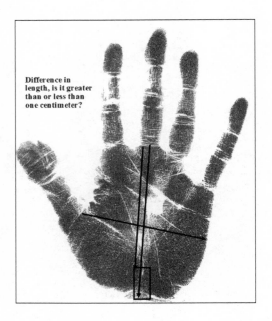

Difference in length, is it greater than or less than one centimeter?

Here are the summaries of the measurements to determine primary element:

- Short fingers, square palm = Earth
- Short fingers, long palm = Fire
- Long fingers, square palm = Air
- Long fingers, long palm = Water

The secondary element is found in the lines in the palm. If you have ever looked at the lines of your friends, you may have noticed that some people have just a few lines while other people have lots of lines. The texture and thickness of the lines also vary from person to person. These variations also correspond to the four elements.

If you have just a few deep lines in your palm, this represents Earth. If you have lots of fine, delicate lines, this represents Water. If you have deep, numerous lines, this represents Fire. If you have numerous, thin and clear lines, this represents the Air element. Below are some examples so you can see the difference.

By the way, I chose "pure types" for you to look at here, meaning that the primary and secondary element is the same. When you look at most hands, this is not usually the case. Most people have different primary and secondary elements.

Earth Hand and Lines

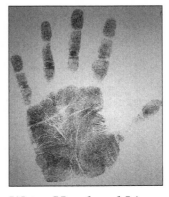

Water Hand and Lines

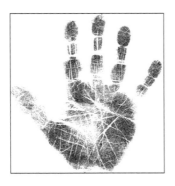

Fire Hand and Lines

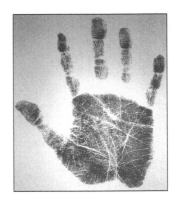

Air Hand and Lines

The last measurement to determine is the strong finger in the hand. I will take you through these with the individual archetypes as we get to them. Stay tuned! For now, all you need to know is that this is what we will be analyzing. Also, it's good for you to know that you may have different strong fingers in your left and your right hands.

Practical Applications

Since each chapter is structured the same way, feel free to jump around and locate the information you need. This book does not need to be read in order, although you may certainly read it that way if you wish. To assist you further, I have three appendixes at the end of this book. Appendix 1 describes a deck of cards that I created called *Palmistry Inspiration Cards*. You may use these cards with the system in this book. I have corresponded the palmistry cards to the Major Arcana cards. These cards are also fun to use as an oracle deck or to learn some basic palmistry in an easy-to-use format.

Appendix 2 lists alphabetically the three types of imbalances: action, emotional and chakras, along with the corresponding archetypes. This appendix is extremely useful if you need to approach the archetype from an imbalance. Rather than having to read through each chapter, the appendix lists the archetypes for you. For example, if you are feeling abandonment issues, work with the Lovers or the World to rebalance that energy. As you get to know the archetypes, it will become easier and easier to know which one to work with when more than one is listed.

Appendix 3 summarizes the palmistry identification for each archetype. Once you learn the system, this appendix will make it easy for you to quickly identify archetypes for yourself and others. You may want to start by identifying your own archetypes and reading those chapters first. Learn the hand measurements and go to the palmistry identification section of the chapter. What if you can't figure out your hand archetype? Sometimes people still struggle in identifying hand characteristics, or they second-guess themselves. I offer a simple archetype identification reading through my web site www.storiesinyour-hands.com.

Let me give you some examples of how to work with this information. Let's say you are having a communication problem with one of your co-workers. As you read through this book, you'll discover aspects of your own archetype and those of your co-worker's. Perhaps you'll recognize a challenging compatibility between you, which may help you relate to your co-worker through the lens of his/her archetype. If your intention is to connect with your co-worker you can begin to do exercises to strengthen his/her archetype in *yourself.* This process sheds light, understanding and appreciation for the way your co-worker functions, enhancing your communication and possibilities around your relationship. You can apply the same techniques to a romantic partner, a parent, a child, or anyone important to you.

Here's another example. Let's say you discover that your archetype is the Moon. By reading the chapter on the Moon, you feel that you may have an imbalance, with too much energy in your archetype. One way for you to rebalance yourself could be to start working with the opposite archetype, which in this case is the Tower. It's important to be your own archetype, but also to weave in your opposite, especially if your energy is in excess. The Tower can introduce aspects of honesty and enlightenment, whereas the Moon emphasizes the subconscious and flowing within cycles. You could further look at this archetype, the Moon, and discover that it relates to the sacral chakra. To balance this chakra, work with other archetypes that also correlate to the sacral, including the Empress, Lovers, Temperance or Star, depending on what you would like to bring into your life specifically. All these archetypes connect with the sacral chakra. For example, if you seem to be unrealistic about your relationships, you would probably want to work with the Lovers or with Temperance. If you're unrealistic about your skills and talents, then work with the Star, which clarifies and gives hope and new purpose. Everyone can benefit in different ways within each archetype.

Another way to use the information is to pull out the Major Arcana cards in your own tarot deck. Shuffle the cards and pick one out of the deck in whatever way you normally choose. As you're shuffling, ask the universe either through your thoughts or out loud, "What archetype do I need to connect to today to assist me the most with my upcoming day?" Then, read the chapter on that archetype and do the exercises. Or if you have a specific problem that you're trying to solve, you could ask the cards about which archetype could assist you the most with solving the problem. Some people like to work with inverted cards. In other words, the meaning varies depending on whether you draw the card upright or upside-down. If you decide to work with inverted cards, you could look at an inverted archetype as being too strong or too weak depending on how you word your question. For example, if you asked the question "What energy do I need to release?" and the Devil came up inverted, you would know that you need to release fear and worry or increase fun and play. The chapters explain the imbalances for each archetype.

Keep a record of your main archetypes in a daily journal. You'll find that the more you work with the energy of the archetypes, the more in sync you will feel with your own authentic destiny. In order to be yourself, you first need to know yourself. The information in this book will give you a new perspective that you can work with every day, adding new insights and bringing a new sense of freedom and joy to your daily routine!

A Note to Professional Coaches, Counselors, Psychologists and Energy Healers

While it is my intention that anyone may pick up this book and use it without any prior experience either in tarot or palmistry, I would like to point out that this material is also invaluable for the professional. Palmistry can interface with a wide range of other modalities, complimenting or supplementing a variety of professional practices. I offer further information and trainings, so please contact me or visit www.worldofhands.com or www.storiesinyourhands.com. If you are already a professional palm reader, I truly hope that you see the value of this information, that it may give you a new perspective to include in your readings and further empower your clients. For the professional tarot reader, I hope that you choose to include the palm in your readings to assist your clients in a more tangible way. I find that people generally do recognize their archetypes and enjoy discovering a new way to align themselves authentically, regardless of what else is discussed in their particular reading.

Now let's all go on a journey…

Chapter 0

0–The Fool

*"A journey of a thousand miles begins
with a single step."* — Lao Tzu

MY FOOL'S JOURNEY BEGAN WITH A TRIP TO THE library back in 2008. I was wandering through the aisles that day, which is not something I normally do, and I ended up in front of the metaphysical section. Some of the books in front of me were about dreams, past lives, angels, numerology, spell casting, and astrology. The book I picked up was about palmistry. It's cover, emblazoned by a large energetic hand, caught my attention. It was Johnny Fincham's, *Palmistry: Apprentice to Pro in 24 Hours*. I thought to myself that I knew absolutely nothing about this subject and wasn't even sure I wanted to. Like many others, I am guessing, I assumed that palmistry was mostly made up stuff about your length of life, how many children you were going to have, and very little more than that. But I decided to take a chance and bring it home, excited to read something new. I didn't know it at the time, but that single, seemingly small event marked the beginning of my new life. It opened me to an entirely new world that eventually shaped my career and life purpose, assisting others in discovering deep truths about themselves.

Physical Attributes

Oh no! You might be thinking; *I must be an idiot if I'm the Fool.* What you need to know about the archetypes is that they all have wonderful qualities, even the ones with "negative" connotations. The Fool is also known as the Jester. Physically, he represents youth or child-like innocence. You do not actually have to be a child to be in touch with the Fool. Anytime you tap into your inner child, you connect to aspects of the Fool. In the tarot card, the Fool is depicted in yellow and brown garb. The yellow represents the sunny disposition of youth, while browns symbolize a journey or adventure. To express the Fool's energy, wear clothes that make you feel young, open your eyes wide, and be relaxed and carefree.

Emotional Attributes

The Fool is all about connecting with your inner child. Emotionally this involves trust and knowing that you are completely supported by the universe. The Fool does not worry about outcomes or consequences. It's about being in an innocent state. Here we see him at the edge of a cliff, unconcerned with danger.

Mental Attributes

Mentally, the Fool is not analytical, but rather open and curious, like the wide-eyed child who is exploring and learning something new. He is holding a white flower delicately in one hand, as if just freshly plucked from the grass nearby.

Spiritual Attributes

Spiritually, the Fool is innocent and carefree, choosing to live in the moment and be open to possibilities. He is easily influenced by others. He is beginning a journey, as we can determine from the sack of belongings behind his shoulder.

Key Words for the Fool

Curious, beginnings, fun, adventure, innocence, trust, infinite possibilities, worry free

Palmistry Identification of the Fool

Water + Apollo

In the hands, the Fool is represented by the following combination: long fingers, long palm, Water, and long Apollo, or ring finger. Apollo is named after the Roman God of the Sun. When we look at finger lengths, we are comparing them against each other. Apollo is measured against the index finger, or Jupiter. When Apollo is ½ centimeter longer than Jupiter or more, it is considered long. Strength of a finger is also determined by the thickness of the finger and how straight it is. A straight finger is always stronger than a bent one and a thicker finger is stronger than a thinner one. Of course, the little finger will always be thinner. How I would like to train your eye is to look at the fingers relative to each other. A very strong Apollo finger will be nearly as long as the middle finger, thick and straight compared to other fingers. Here are hand print examples of the Fool archetype:

The Fool Hand Print Example 1

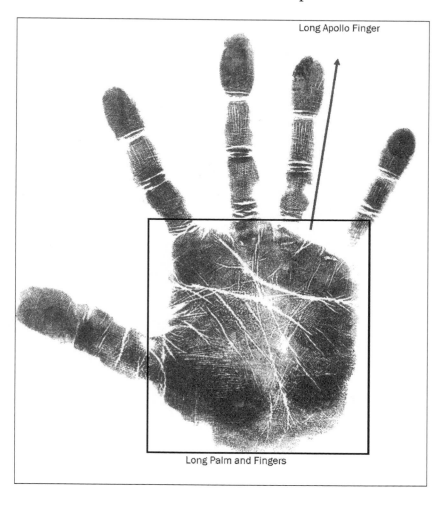

Long Apollo Finger

Long Palm and Fingers

The Fool Hand Print Example 2

Examples & Exercises

There are ways to align with and balance all of the arche-types. Refer to this section in each of the chapters to balance and heal the energy of the specific archetype.

Mudra

To tap into the Fool archetype with a mudra, place your palms up in a relaxed and open position with the little fin-gers touching and the edge of the hands (called the percussion) touching each other.

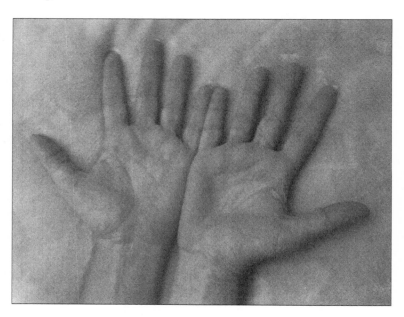

Questions for Growth and Coaches Tips

1. How can I reconnect to my inner child? Working with the growth questions can open up so much potential for you. For the inner child, think about what you used to do when you were actually a child. I used to make perfume and try to sell it door-to-door. Another time I

unknowingly made wine under my bed after smashing up some grapes and letting them ferment there for a couple of weeks.

2. How can I be more trusting? Trust levels are easy to recognize when you compare them with how much control you feel you need to have in any given situation, or with a particular person. If you're a control "freak," you don't trust enough.

3. How can I let go of stress and seriousness? Stress has many ways to release. Some of my favorite ways are through physical movement. Dancing or exercising can be fun and playful.

4. How would I like to play right now? If you take a break every hour to stretch and breathe, you will actually be more productive overall. When you check in with your body, it allows you to be more present. It's also fun to experiment with turning mundane tasks into play. Think of everything like a game and see how your attitude shifts. I like to think about driving a car in this way. Sometimes I'll pretend I'm in a video game.

5. What can I allow into my life? For allowing something into your life, look at what's missing, then ask yourself why it's missing. Sometimes all you need is to reprioritize your day or week a little bit. For example, if you want more abundance in your life, think about what makes you feel abundant. I recommend keeping an amount of cash in your purse or wallet that helps you feel this abundant mindset. Then, when you need to buy something, even if you end up paying with a credit or debit card, you feel more prosperous because you have cash.

Truth Statements for the Fool

1. I trust in the universe to provide all that I need.

2. It's ok for me to still be learning and growing.
3. I am in touch with my inner child and innocence.
4. I am connected fully to the present moment.
5. I let go of worry and stress.

Chakra Association

Root

Identifying Imbalances

Too much Fool is represented by the victim, who is taken advantage of and unaware of what's going on around him. This includes making foolish choices and later regretting them. Too little Fool is taking life too seriously, not being light-hearted, or falling into depression. If you can't remember what it was like to be a kid, you are definitely deficient in the Fool.

The Fool at Home

The Fool at home is fun to be around. He tells jokes, laughs and plays games. Home is a little bit messy, but it feels cozy and warm. The Fool enjoys having animals around because they remind him of himself, especially dogs. We see him with a white dog in the card's picture.

The Fool at Work

The Fool at work prefers a loose structure. He is very creative, and not happy being confined to strict routines. He needs plenty of breaks and fresh air during the day to stay motivated. He is easy to work with and does well in groups. He prefers not to take the lead on projects or to be in charge.

The Fool in Relationships

The Fool is curious and loves to experiment. He is open to non-traditional relationships that feel good. He hates confinement of any kind. He is in touch with his feelings in the moment, but doesn't worry or over-think them. He is kind and generous with his time and affections and expects the same in return. He is naïve about the complexity of emotions and how they affect others.

Best Compatibility

Empress, Strength, Devil

Good Compatibility

Hermit, Wheel of Fortune, Temperance, Star, Judgement

Challenging Compatibility

Emperor, Chariot, Tower, Sun, World

Opposite Archetype

Chariot

Famous Fool Archetypes

Mother Theresa, Pierce Brosnan, Cameron Diaz, Marilyn Monroe, Heidi Klum, Bilbo Baggins, Peter Pan

Chapter 1

1–The Magician

"What you get by achieving your goals is not as important as what you become by achieving your goals." — Henry David Thoreau

I RECENTLY CONNECTED WITH THE MAGICIAN AF-
ter a couple of months of daily, hour-long meditation. I've
known that meditation is healthy in so many ways, by reducing stress, balancing brain waves, getting more oxygen into
our bodies through deeper breathing, and improving overall
health. I wasn't trying to create these things; they simply arise
as side effects of meditating. At the time, I was working on my
self-worth to improve my relationships. Anyway, I wasn't seeing
any noticeable results from my meditating, at least in my mind,
so I decided to ask the universe for a sign. Now a sign could be
anything, but I wanted a sign that was special for me. I happen
to be a fan of roses. They are beautiful and fragrant and they
make a space feel more special. I asked for my sign to be red or
pink roses. Then I went about my business.

The very next day, I was at a ski sale shopping for a new pair
of goggles for the upcoming ski season. I proceeded to a table
covered by at least 100 pairs of loose, shiny goggles. After trying
a few on without any enthusiasm, the salesman noticed a pair
off to the side, still in their box. He said, "Here's another pair
of the brand you're looking for, but it looks like there might be
some kind of graphic on the strap."

As he pulled the goggles out of their box, the strap did not
have the usual company logo. Instead, it had a lovely design of
red and pink roses! I knew this was my sign from the universe
and of course, this is the pair that I ended up with. Since that
day, I see red or pink roses everywhere, nearly every day in so
many creative ways. They always make me smile.

Physical Attributes

The Magician represents a young person or someone young
at heart. He is wearing clothes of the alchemist, whatever he
needs to wear to create his reality. He is comfortable and relaxed.
He wears the red robe of passion and desire and a white tunic
underneath, representing his purity of intention. I recommend

that you wear outfits that embody in some way who you want to become. For example, I saw a news piece once about a young boy, about ten years old, who wore a three piece suit every day to school. The suit wasn't a required uniform and no one else in this school dressed this way except for him. When an interviewer asked him why he wore it, he replied that he was going to be president of the United States one day so he wanted to look the part and prepare himself for that role right now.

Emotional Attributes

The Magician is determined and able. He first feels the energy of what he is about to create. For example, if he is creating a loving relationship, he feels the love within himself first. He is holding a wand to the sky in his right hand and his left hand is pointing down to the ground, signifying his emotional connection to heaven and earth. Feel your desire right now as if it's already come true. This should immediately put you in a state of gratitude. Gratitude opens the doorway to manifesting your desires more quickly and easily.

Mental Attributes

The Magician is the alchemist, mentally focusing on the outcome first. This is why he has the infinity symbol above his head. You are a powerful creator. Take some time to explore potential outcomes.

Spiritual Attributes

Spiritually, the Magician is the manifestor. He knows God (or the Universe, if you prefer) is already in all things. He is converting the energy of God into matter. He has all the tools he needs at his disposal. On the table is a pentacle, a sword and a cup. He is holding a wand. These are the suits of the Minor Arcana. Around him are red and white flowers, the same colors as his attire. If God is in all things and God is in you, then you are in all things too. Since you are in all things, you can attract all things to you. Choose wisely.

Key Words for the Magician

Manifest, create, magic, alchemy, attract

Palmistry Identification

Fire + Mercury

In the hands, the Magician is represented by the following combination: short fingers, long palm, Fire, and long little finger. This finger is called Mercury, named after the Roman God of communication. To tell if the Mercury finger is long, place it next to Apollo. It is long if it rises above the upper phalange of Apollo. This finger can be a bit tricky sometimes, though, because it is often what is called "low-set," especially in women's hands. A low-set Mercury will begin ¾ to 1 cm lower on the palm than Apollo. In other words, it will look slightly out of place next to the other fingers. When this occurs, add back in about ½ cm of length to determine if it's actually long or not, because it will naturally appear short when it's low-set. Please see the second example to understand this. Here are hand print examples of the Magician archetype:

The Magician Hand Print Example 1

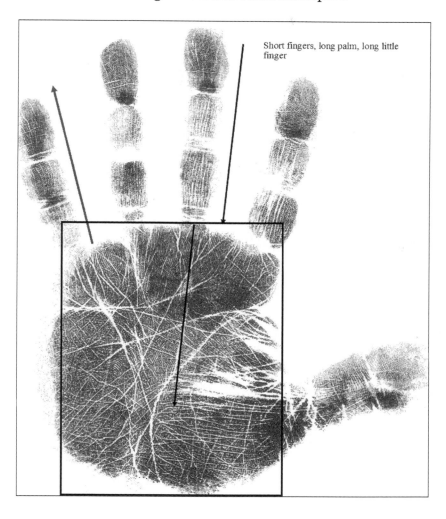

Short fingers, long palm, long little finger

Magician Hand Print Example 2 (note
the low-setting of Mercury)

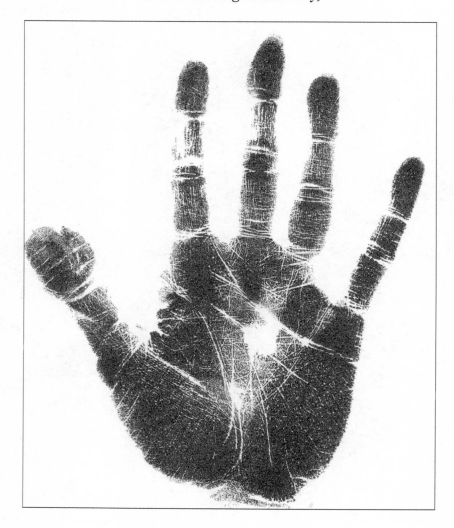

Examples and Exercises

Mudra

Place your palms facing up and side by side. Touch your left thumb to your left index finger and your right thumb to your right index finger.

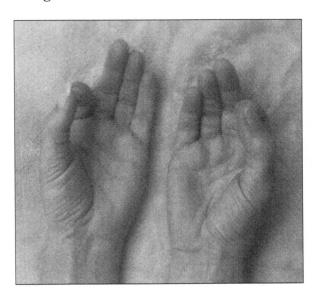

Questions for Growth and Coaches Tips

1. What do I wish to create? This may be viewed from many perspectives, including, for example, your physical body. While you may not be able to grow taller (or can you?), it is possible to have erect posture to give the impression of height. You may wish for more joy. Take a look at what actually brings you joy first. I receive joy from the mountains. When I was a little girl, my family traveled to the plains in the central part of the United States. My mother said I looked around and asked, "Where are the

mountains?" They have been part of my surroundings my entire life and I treasure them.

2. What resources do I need to create what I want in my life? With this question, it's important to look at what you are currently able to accomplish on your own. Take a look at what you can delegate to free up your time for more important things. For example, I delegate my accounting to someone who loves it. It's a winning situation for both of us.

3. What feeling do I need to express in order to create what I want in my life? Identify this feeling, then go to it as often as possible during your day. For instance, if you want to attract love into your life, be loving toward others and yourself.

4. How can I simplify my life to be more in alignment with my goals and desires? Examine how complicated your life is and what responsibilities you are claiming that really don't belong to you. For example, many people struggle with worrying and fretting about their children. Does this really serve them or you? What if you let that go, or consciously replace moments of worry with the joy or love they bring to your life?

5. What person, place or thing do I need to connect with that resonates at the same vibration as my desire? This question is to get you thinking about energies that already exist, either around you or somewhere else in the world. Pick a specific desire and ask yourself where its manifestation already exists. Maybe it's a famous person, living or dead, or a special place you have visited. Then go into the mudra and tune into it.

Truth Statements for the Magician

1. I am able to create the life I want.

2. Creating is easy and fun.
3. I see and feel what I want before it comes into my reality.
4. I release negative influences that interfere with my ability to create.
5. I am a magical manifestor.

Chakra Association

Solar Plexus, Crown

Identifying Imbalances

Too much Magician results in manipulation. It may also show up as having too many plans without any clear follow through. Too little Magician is scattered energy, foggy and unfocused, having no plans at all.

The Magician at Home

At home, the Magician knows just where to put everything. It is not necessarily clean and tidy, but he is aware of the location of everything and can find anything easily. He has lots of magical items to help him. He's a gadget guy.

The Magician at Work

At work, the Magician is methodical, yet quick. He has thousands of ideas and just loves to brainstorm. His desk is full of papers and notes. He works best alone, then passing along his ideas to be completed by delegates. He doesn't have the patience to complete everything. It's the excitement of starting something new that keeps his passions burning.

The Magician in Relationships

The Magician gets bored easily. He needs a partner who cannot only keep up with him mentally, but also someone who is exciting and fun herself. He would do well with a partner who can ground him somewhat and bring some stability to his life. Passion rules the relationship.

Best Compatibility

Emperor, Chariot, Wheel of Fortune, Sun

Good Compatibility

Hanged Man, Tower, World

Challenging Compatibility

High Priestess, Hierophant, Hermit, Justice, Moon, Judgement

Opposite Archetype

Justice

Famous Magician Archetypes

Albert Einstein, Tom Hanks, Bill Clinton, JK Rowling, Max Planck, Marlene Dietrich, Gandalf, Merlin

Chapter 2

2–The High Priestess

"Eyes that look are common; eyes that see
are rare." — J. Oswald Sanders

I CONNECTED WITH THE HIGH PRIESTESS ON THE day after my fortuitous visit to the library. As I started to read the palmistry book I'd checked out, I had a strange and familiar feeling come over me, like I already knew the material, even though I had never studied it at all in this lifetime. It felt like running into an old friend whose name you can't remember, but know that you have been friends before, even if you can't place when or where. I was suddenly getting flickering images of China and France and a strong message that I needed to learn this material again. The deeper I got into the book, the stronger this impression became. If you have never experienced déjà vu before in your lifetime, I can only tell you that when it happens, it makes you question reality as you know it, and it can change everything.

Physical Attributes

The High Priestess is a beautiful, virginal woman. She is dressed in white robes of purity and the blue shawl of intuition. Wear clothes that make you feel pure and wholesome. Try dressing simply in white or solid colors. If you normally wear jewelry, take it off for a day, including your watch.

Emotional Attributes

The High Priestess is emotionally calm, serene and outwardly cool. She purposefully keeps herself detached from others in order to stay connected to her own intuition. Feel this calm tranquility in your own body by taking a few deep breaths. Mindful breathing is a way to turn your attention inward and reset your system. It's a great tool and only takes a few seconds.

Mental Attributes

Her crown has a large, spherical center with two points facing outward, indicating her mental balance between left and right brain, and a strong intuitive centeredness. Pay attention to your inner voice. Try doing this for an entire day. What it is telling you? Do you listen to it or ignore it?

Spiritual Attributes

Spiritually, the High Priestess is connected to her higher self. The crescent moon at her feet shows that she is deeply committed to growth and following her own pathway. The cross on her chest shows that she is religious and identifies with a formal practice. Whether you are religious or not is not important. To be in alignment with the High Priestess, it is only necessary to tune into your inner self and seek your own counsel.

Key Words for the High Priestess

Pure, subconscious, intuitive, cloistered, tranquil, calm, deep

Palmistry Identification

Water + Mercury

The hand shape of the High Priestess is Water, long fingers and rectangular palm, and a long little finger, Mercury. Here are some hand print examples of the High Priestess archetype:

High Priestess Hand Print Example 1

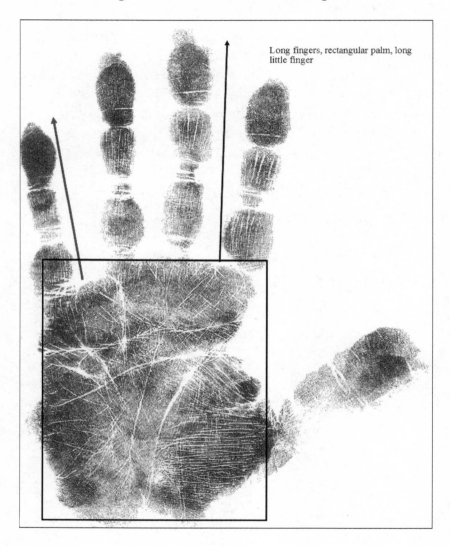

Long fingers, rectangular palm, long little finger

High Priestess Hand Print Example 2

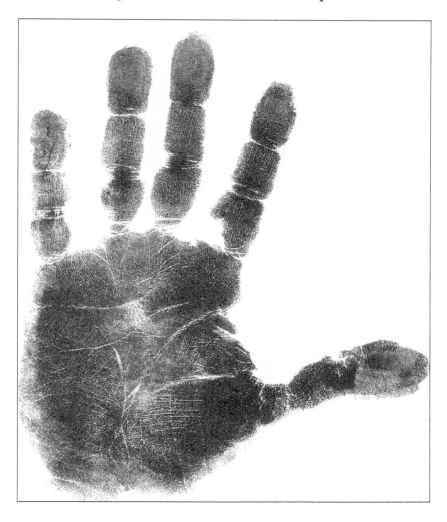

Examples and Exercises

Mudra

   With the palms facing each other, bend the middle, ring and little fingers down on both hands, touching each other from the middle phalange. Point the index fingers straight and touch the tips of these fingers together. Have the thumbs relaxed and gently facing outward.

Questions for Growth and Coaches Tips

   1. How does my inner voice speak to me? Pay attention to all of your senses. Your intuitive senses are also called "clairs," after the French word for *clear,* of which clair-voyance is the most well known, meaning clear seeing. This is about paying attention to visions. But you may

also receive information through feelings (clairsentience), hearing (clairaudience), thoughts (claircognizance), smells (clairalience), and tastes (clairambience.)

2. How can I spend more time listening to my inner voice? This requires setting aside time to be in quiet stillness. It's much harder to get messages in a noisy, frazzled environment. I recommend tuning in early in the morning or just before bed. These are the two times of day when your brain is more relaxed and the outside world is also calmer and less active.

3. What imbalances do I have regarding my intuition? If you have repetitive negative thoughts or feelings, this will throw you off balance. For example, many people feel they're not good enough. If you feel this way, you're more likely to doubt your intuition and second guess yourself.

4. How can I strengthen my intuition? One way is to make a commitment to start working with your archetypes. Recording your impressions in a journal or clearing clutter from your physical spaces are also wonderful ways. There are many answers to this question. It's important to know that everyone has intuitive abilities, including you. Think of your intuition like a muscle. It needs to be worked out in order to fine tune it.

5. How can I place myself in an emotionally serene state right now? Deep breathing and being grateful for something is a great start. Turn off the television or light a candle. Take a hot bubble bath. Look at the stars or the clouds.

Truth Statements for the High Priestess

1. I am committed to developing my intuition.
2. I balance my inner and outer worlds.

3. I take time to check in with my inner voice before making decisions.
4. I surrender to the flow of the universe.
5. I am calm, balanced and serene.

Chakra Association

Third Eye

Identifying Imbalances

Too much High Priestess is withdrawn from the outside world, keeping her wisdom locked up inside herself. Too little High Priestess results in a cold delivery of information and an inability to connect with and understand others.

The High Priestess at Home

The High Priestess has a minimalist space. She is neither extravagant nor cluttered. Her kitchen is full of healthy food. She does not partake in alcohol or drugs, since this would affect her intuitive abilities. She prefers peace and quiet around her and spends a lot of her time in meditation and contemplation. She stays away from crowds and noisy surroundings as much as possible.

The High Priestess at Work

At work, the High Priestess prefers going with the flow of her moods and emotions. She prefers to work alone in a quiet and tranquil space. Writing suits her, or consulting with clients one-on-one. She is better off in a flexible schedule and working for herself.

The High Priestess in Relationships

In relationships, the High Priestess takes her time in choosing the best partner for herself. She needs someone who honors her feminine nature and allows her to be herself. She needs a fair amount of time to herself, her independence is important to her. She enjoys quiet evenings indoors with her partner.

Best Compatibility

Hermit, Hierophant, Death, Star, Moon

Good Compatibility

Strength, Judgement, World

Challenging Compatibility

Magician, Lovers, Chariot, Devil, Tower

Opposite Archetype

Lovers

Famous High Priestess Archetypes

Barack Obama, Frederic Chopin, Jennifer Lopez, Lyndon Johnson, Heidi Klum, Queen Elizabeth II, Albus Dumbledore

Chapter 3

3–The Empress

"One learns people through the heart, not the eyes or the intellect." — Mark Twain

MY MOTHER IS MY CONNECTION TO THE EMPRESS.
I remember the time in my life when I got my wisdom teeth pulled. Since they were impacted, I had to have oral surgery when I was nineteen years old. I was still living at home back then while attending college, and my mother was in charge of tending to my needs while I recovered. It was spring break of my sophomore year. I remember being very groggy and helpless for about three days. She would periodically come into my room, replace the bloody gauzes in my mouth and bring me liquids and soft foods. She would help me get out of bed and let me lean on her to get to the bathroom. I was completely safe and supported in her care.

Physical Attributes

The Empress has quite a different look than the High Priestess. In this tarot card, we see a beautiful woman seated on a comfortable cushion. She has a loose white dress with red flowers, she may even be pregnant. She is outside near a forest with healthy grass growing beneath her feet. The symbol for the female is beneath her seat. For yourself, dress in loose and comfortable clothes, whatever makes you feel relaxed.

Emotional Attributes

Emotionally, the Empress is generous and nurturing. When you're in a space of true giving, you're in a space of abundance instead of lack. Feel what it's like to have more than you need, so much so that you desire to share.

Mental Attributes

Mentally, the Empress represents abundance. She is fertile with growth all around her. She takes her time in planting ideas and letting them grow. Ask yourself what you would like to see grow around you.

Spiritual Attributes

The Empress is spiritually connected to the earth and nature. Plants and animals thrive around her. She helps others
grow through her nurturing presence. Spend some time in a
garden or go out and buy some flowers. Appreciate their beauty.

Key Words for the Empress

Fertility, nurturing, abundant, growth, nature

Palmistry Identification

Earth + Saturn

In the hands, the Empress is represented by the following
combination: short fingers, square palm, Earth, and long middle
finger. This finger is called Saturn, named after the Roman God
of the harvest. To know if Saturn is long, see how it compares
to its closest fingers, the ring and the index. If neither of these
fingers reaches half way into the upper phalange of Saturn, then
Saturn is long. Here are hand print examples of the Empress
archetype:

Empress Hand Print Example 1

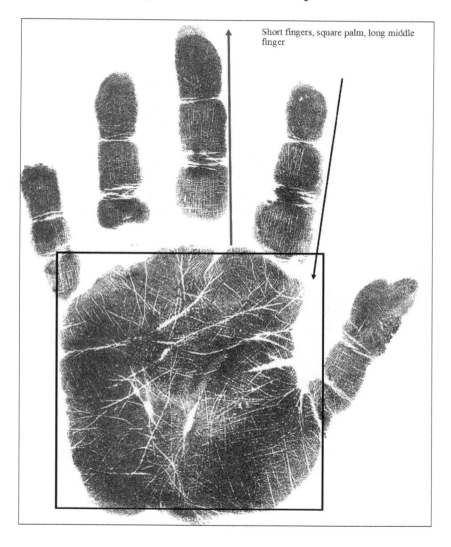

Short fingers, square palm, long middle finger

Empress Hand Print Example 2

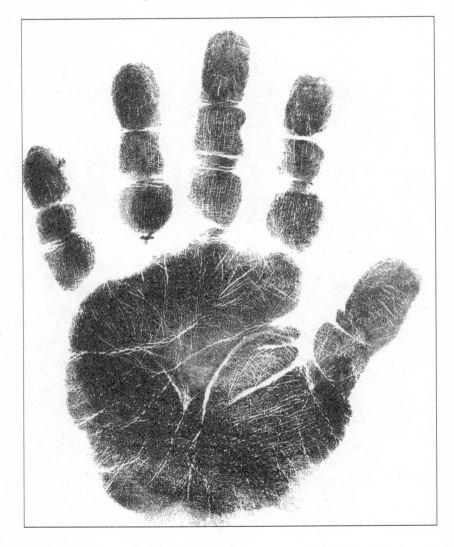

Examples and Exercises

Mudra

With your palms open and facing up, bend your middle finger and place it on your thumb ball region of your hand.

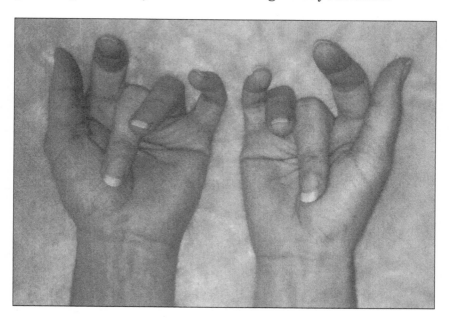

Questions for Growth and Coaches Tips

1. How does scarcity show up in my life? This question forces you to look at areas in your life that need healing. Pay attention to conversations where you find yourself or others complaining or blaming. Ultimately, you are one hundred percent responsible for your life and your beliefs create your reality. If you are blaming someone else for something, turn it around and look instead at what belief in yourself created this circumstance. Forgive yourself for the situation and see how your life shifts.

2. What brings me joy? Define joy first in order to attract more of it. It's different for everyone. Think of things that are healthy for you rather than unhealthy. For example, if you love vodka and believe it brings you joy, is this a healthy association for you? Make a healthier choice, like carrot juice, and begin to associate joy with it every time you drink it.

3. In what ways can I be more emotionally generous? As you give joyfully, this elevates everyone and everything around you. Practice saying hello to every person on a hiking trail, or go out of your way to open a door for someone else. Notice and celebrate the reactions you'll receive.

4. What does abundance mean to me? Look at this in seven key areas of your life: personal, financial, career, health, relationships, fun and service. Get specific with numbers and time frames, yet stay detached of the outcome. I like to use the phrase "or something better." This helps attract abundance into your reality in ways you might not even be able to imagine.

5. Who and how do I like to nurture? Define your own nurturing style. Do you like to bake pies, experiment with essential oils, take hot bubble baths? It's ok to look at ways to nurture yourself as well as others. For example, I used to own a restaurant, and today I still enjoy cooking for others.

Truth Statements for the Empress

1. I am lavish abundance.
2. I enjoy being emotionally generous.
3. I love to go out into nature.
4. I allow myself to nourish myself.
5. Love is everywhere and in all things.

Chakra Association

Sacral, Heart

Identifying Imbalances

Too much Empress is represented by over-mothering or smothering energy that doesn't allow growth from the recipient, like over-watering a plant. Too little Empress shows up as scarcity and barrenness.

The Empress at Home

The home of the Empress is full of luxuries. It's large and spacious, yet cozy and warm. Her fridge is full of food, especially fruits and vegetables. She is welcoming and gracious with guests. It's a place you want to come back to again and again.

The Empress at Work

At work, the Empress is diplomatic. She doesn't choose to fight or argue, but seeks solutions that benefit everyone involved. She takes her time in her work to make sure it's done properly. The Empress prefers to be outside in nature and connecting with it in some way. She also doesn't mind working alone with plants or animals.

The Empress in Relationships

The Empress is emotionally generous. She loves to give massages and luxurious affection to her partner. She enjoys cooking and dining, preferably with organic food. She is very committed in a relationship once she chooses a partner.

Best Compatibility

Fool, Lovers, Wheel of Fortune

Good Compatibility

Justice, Death, Temperance, Star, Moon, Sun, World

Challenging Compatibility

Strength, Devil, Tower

Opposite Archetype

Devil

Famous Empress Archetypes

Charlie Sheen, Fairy Godmother, Snow White

Chapter 4

4–The Emperor

"The price of greatness is responsibility." — Winston Churchill

MY CONNECTION TO THE EMPEROR ARCHETYPE always reminds me of my father. I was the youngest of four children and my father was an electrical engineer. He always worked very hard to make sure that his family's needs were met. Not one to say much, he showed us through his actions how important we were to him. I still remember Sunday afternoons when I was a little girl. My dad would take me out to get an ice cream cone and we would enjoy it together, just the two of us. It was our special time together. We enjoyed rocky road, burnt almond fudge, butter pecan, strawberry and bubble gum. Dad's home was his castle and we lived in the same house for my entire childhood. In fact, my parents still live in that same house today.

Physical Attributes

The Magician is matured as the Emperor in the fourth Major Arcana card. Here we see an elderly man with a beard, dressed in red and sitting on his throne. The age represents his wisdom, the throne his success and leadership. The mountains in the background show his power and groundedness. For you to be in touch with the Emperor, dress in clothes that make you feel strong and powerful. For example, wear nice fabric or fine jewelry. Sit up straight in your chair or stand tall and proud.

Emotional Attributes

The Emperor is always in control of his emotions. He only reveals what he feels is beneficial to reveal for himself and his empire. He does not want to show weakness of any kind. For yourself, what makes you feel powerful?

Mental Attributes

The Emperor is ambitious, having used his mental strength to follow through on his desires and ambitions. He is mentally sharp and calculating. Mentally focus on the long-term and long-lasting in your own life.

Spiritual Attributes

Spiritually, the Emperor is only concerned with foundation. He practices whatever will make him stronger and bring him more power. Create a domain for yourself, or imagine it in your mind, a spiritual palace where you can regain your strength and groundedness.

Key Words for the Emperor

Grounded, stable, foundation, long-lasting, powerful

Palmistry Identification

Earth + Jupiter

In the hands, the Emperor is represented by the following combination: short fingers, square palm, Earth, and long index finger, Jupiter. This finger is named after the Roman God of the Gods. To know if Jupiter is long, see how it compares to the ring finger, Apollo. If it is longer than Apollo, it is considered long. Here are hand print examples of the Emperor archetype:

Emperor Hand Print Example 1

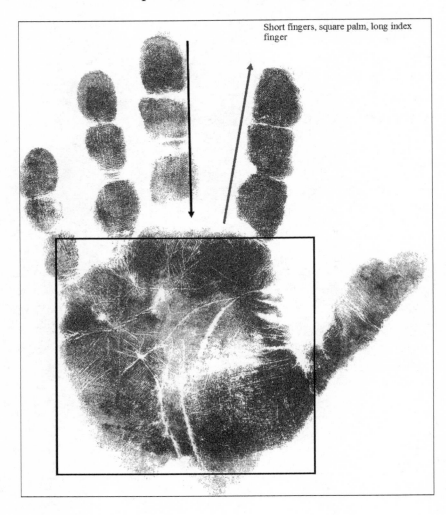

Short fingers, square palm, long index finger

Emperor Hand Print Example 2

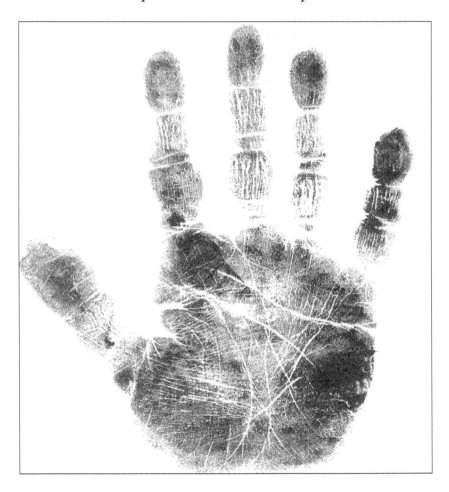

Examples and Exercises

Mudra

Place the hands with the palms facing up. Curl the index finger down so that it touches the thumb ball region. Do this for both hands.

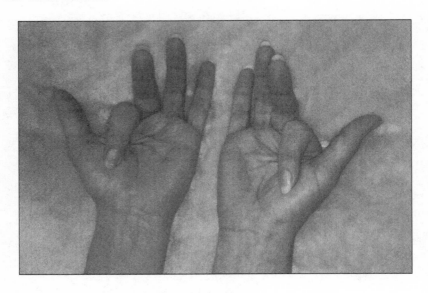

Questions for Growth and Coaches Tips

1. What do I want to create that will last the rest of my life and beyond? This question gets you thinking about your legacy, what's truly important to you, and how it may outlive you. I want to create a new way of thinking about the hands that helps millions of people connect to their authentic destinies.
2. What is my domain? You can have more than one. For one person, it might be a family. For another, it might be heading up a big company.
3. In all areas of my life, how can I make my vision bigger? It's not enough to say "I want more money." This isn't

specific enough. How much, by when and for what bigger purpose? Measurable and specific goals become more tangible.

4. What is the greatest expression of myself? This is to help you connect with that divine spark that is already inside you, wanting to leak out. Knowing who you really are is essential in answering this question.

5. What bold step can I take today to get me closer to my vision? If you don't show up, you essentially block it from being able to happen. You must get a little bit out of your comfort zone and stretch yourself in order to grow. Change is growth; get comfortable with change and you will live a more fulfilling life.

Truth Statements for the Emperor

1. I easily set my goals and follow through.
2. I take my time with setting a thorough foundation.
3. I am strong and powerful.
4. I am able and willing to create the life I want.
5. I use my power and influence to help myself and others.

Chakra Association

Root, Solar Plexus

Identifying Imbalances

Too much Emperor is the dictator. Too little Emperor is a weak foundation with no staying power.

The Emperor at Home

The Emperor has a well-built, large home with all the comforts inside it. He delegates its upkeep to housekeepers so he can focus on more important matters.

The Emperor at Work

The Emperor is the ruler of his dominion. Whatever area of work he decides to take on, it is better for everyone if he is in full command. It's not that he doesn't take advice or allow others in on a project, as long as he retains the final say as to how and what gets done.

The Emperor in Relationships

The Emperor makes a stable partner, but he is not always emotionally available. He values his time to himself, and only welcomes you in when he is feeling good about his work and progress in life. When things are going well, he loves to share the finer things in life with someone special.

Best Compatibility

Magician, Chariot, Justice

Good Compatibility

Lovers, Strength, Hermit, Devil, World

Challenging Compatibility

Fool, Wheel of Fortune, Temperance, Devil, Tower

Opposite Archetype

Temperance

Famous Emperor Archetypes

Michael Jordan, Donald Trump, Vladimir Putin, Russell Wilson, Osama bin Laden, Prince Charles, Aslan

Chapter 5

5–The Hierophant

"An investment in knowledge pays the best
interest." — Benjamin Franklin

I BELIEVE THERE IS TRUTH IN THE SAYING THAT when the student is ready, the teacher appears. My own Hierophant appeared in 2000 as a wise woman Qigong instructor from Switzerland. Qigong (pronounced chee-gung) is the ancient Chinese study and cultivation of energy, or life force. This energy refers to the "vital force" behind all things in the universe within the human body. Qigong is over 5,000 years old. The practice incorporates movements, breathing, sounds and visualizations. There are over 7,000 forms of Qigong including tai chi. It is a system for improving and maintaining overall health and wellness. It is especially good for reducing stress, increasing balance, building energy and maintaining the vitality of the internal organs.

As a result of this ancient training, I have reaped many benefits. For example, I used to have lots of allergies, including allergies to dogs, cats, dust and bees. I used to carry an epinephrine shot with me wherever I went. After practicing Qigong for a while on a weekly basis, my allergies disappeared. You may think that there was another reason for this, but there was nothing else I was doing differently.

I also had a skiing accident a few years ago where I twisted my knee in some avalanche debris. It took me about fifteen minutes to dig myself out, my ski didn't release, and no one could help me because I was on a quiet run where no one else was around. My knee swelled up and I was worried that I would not be able to ski the rest of the season. It was February. I decided that I would use Qigong to help myself, so when I got home I put an ice pack on my knee, put my leg up and envisioned green light coming through my hands into my knee. I did this for several hours a day for four days. I also focused positive thoughts on my knee like "my knee is perfectly healthy." By the fifth day, my knee was back to normal and I was back up on the mountain again. To this day, I never had any more trouble with that knee.

Physical Attributes

The Hierophant card is also known as the High Priest. He is shown in red and white, sitting above his followers. Physically, he is the elderly scholar, sitting strong and proud to set the example for others. For yourself, try wearing something from an elder or ancestor that has significance to you.

Emotional Attributes

Emotionally, the Hierophant has controlled emotions. It would not be proper to show too much emotion, so he keeps his own feelings inside. This does not mean, however, that he does not feel deeply. He does, but he expresses himself in a controlled and parental type fashion. Ask yourself how a "future you" would feel looking back at your current situation.

Mental Attributes

The Hierophant represents traditional wisdom. He has studied truths of the past and is deeply concerned with carrying on tradition and ancient knowledge. Interview your elders if they're still alive. Ask them what they have learned that's important to share.

Spiritual Attributes

Spiritually, the Hierophant is traditional. He is called to choose a pathway with a rich history and carry it forward to the next generation of believers. He is patient and consistent in this practice. Examine your own traditions and why you have them. Keep the ones that make you feel good and let go of the ones that don't.

Key Words for the Hierophant

Wisdom, tradition, patient, teacher

Palmistry Identification

Air + Saturn

In the hands, the Hierophant is represented by the following combination: long fingers, square palm, Air, and long middle finger, Saturn. Here are hand print examples of the Hierophant archetype:

Hierophant Hand Print Example 1

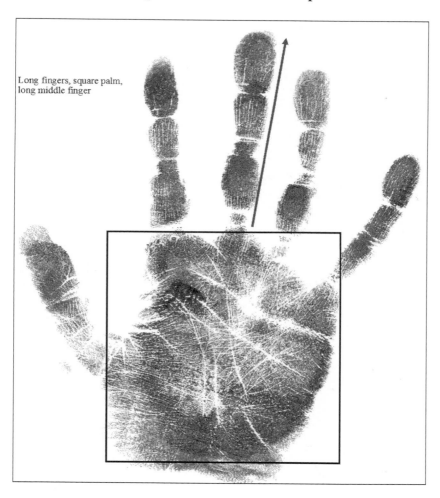

Long fingers, square palm, long middle finger

Hierophant Hand Print Example 2

Examples and Exercises

Mudra

To connect with the Hierophant in a mudra, place your palms facing each other. With straight middle and little fingers, touch these together to opposite hands. Curl all the other fingers and thumbs inward and touch the knuckles together.

Questions for Growth and Coaches Tips

1. What traditions do I feel deeply about? Take some time to examine your own family and extended family. You chose the family you belong to before entering the physical body you now have. Don't just look at events or activities, but look for beliefs that carry through as well.

2. What traditions would I like to carry forward? Make a list of positive and negative traditions. Maybe your grandmother made the best apple pie. Consider making

it for your own family. Maybe you come from a line of alcoholics. This too is here to teach you something. If you notice a particularly destructive pattern in your family, know that you can be the one to break it so that it no longer carries forward into the next generation. Recognizing patterns is the first step.

3. What do I know well that other people ask me about regularly? This will help you get in touch with your inner teacher. Facts you carry inside yourself may seem obvious to you because you already know them, but they are not necessarily obvious to everyone else.

4. What do I enjoy sharing with others? You have knowledge that no one else does. No one on the planet has walked your pathway. This makes you very special and precious. Make sure your masterpiece doesn't stay in the closet.

5. Who do I consider a mentor? What is her message? Look at both living and dead people who have made an impact on you. This may include famous people or simply people you have known over the years.

Truth Statements for the Hierophant

1. I wisely choose which traditions to keep and which to let go of.
2. I enjoy teaching valuable information to others.
3. I am connected to universal wisdom at all times.
4. I use traditions to expand my individuality.
5. I learn from the strength of my ancestors and mentors.

Chakra Association

Throat, Third Eye

Identifying Imbalances

Too much Hierophant is represented by outdated dogma, old information that is unevolved and has outlived its usefulness. It's about holding on to outdated information. Too little Hierophant is represented by foolish choices, blindly ignoring a formula that's already tried and true. It also includes rejecting valuable ancient traditions, such as palmistry or astrology.

The Hierophant at Home

At home, the Hierophant keeps a tight ship. Youngsters are expected to behave and follow the rules of the household. There are formal times throughout the day designated for the family. Dinner is always formal and proper table manners are followed. Cell phones are not allowed at the table. The Hierophant is fair, but firm. Part of the day is spent teaching lessons.

The Hierophant at Work

At work, the Hierophant is always on time, even early. He completes tasks formally and traditionally. He keeps a strict schedule without much variation one day to the next. He respects routine and structure and expects others to do the same. He dislikes innovations unless they are proven to be better than the old systems, and may be slow to embrace them.

The Hierophant in Relationships

The Hierophant makes a loyal and committed partner, but can sometimes fall into the routine category. He likes to know where he stands in the relationship and is willing to work harder if necessary. Although he doesn't show his emotions easily, he expresses his love through his actions and dedication to his partner. He prefers traditional marriage built upon traditional roles.

Best Compatibility

High Priestess, Strength, Justice, Temperance

Good Compatibility

Empress, Lovers, Star, Sun

Challenging Compatibility

Fool, Magician, Hermit, Hanged Man, Devil, Moon

Opposite Archetype

Hermit

Famous Hierophant Archetypes

Leonardo DiCaprio, Justin Timberlake, Muhammad Ali, Mustafa

Chapter 6

6–The Lovers

"Many things will catch your eye, but only a few will catch your heart...pursue those." — Michael Nolan

I HAVE HAD SEVERAL NOTEWORTHY LOVERS throughout my life and I always feel time is richer with a lover by my side. For me, life is more rewarding when I can share all of myself with someone who supports and values me as much as I do him. There is nothing quite like sexual union with another special person. But the Lovers archetype is more than that. When I was younger I valued science and logic. I believed these systems revealed the truth. Growing up with a father who was an electrical engineer and two computer-savvy brothers imprinted my young mind. When I discovered hand analysis, I approached it completely from a scientific perspective, as a language with rules and logical sequencing.

At the same time, however, I was denying an entire spectrum of my being: my intuitive and feminine self. Yes, the stories in your hands do indeed operate within a finite language that can be learned and interpreted. But my true connection to the Lovers came when I finally realized that the story isn't complete unless you add the elements of intuition and superconscious bonds to the equation. Once I integrated this awareness into my analysis, an entirely new level of reading took over, allowing a more complete union with my clients.

Physical Attributes

Here is the first card where we see three beings as opposed to just a single individual. A man and a woman, nude, are standing side by side with an angel above them, bestowing blessings and growth upon their relationship. The nudity represents their purity, sexuality and physical attraction. When we are nude we are essentially exposing ourselves as we are, without pretense. The next time you take a bath or shower, give yourself a few moments to fully appreciate your body.

Emotional Attributes

Emotionally, the Lovers represent loving and passionate energy, emotionally expressive. Know and live your passions to fully understand the Lovers.

Mental Attributes

When you connect with your male and female sides, you are balanced in both logic and intuition, using both in harmony. If you are a "man" hater or "woman" hater, this is a sure sign that a part of you needs healing. The same is true if there is a body part you dislike in yourself. Maybe you love your eyes, but hate your thighs. Learning to love all parts of your body is an important component within this archetype.

Spiritual Attributes

With the presence of the angel in this card along with the two lovers, we are seeing a spiritual oneness through the integration of opposites.

Key Words for the Lovers

Balancing, loving, sexual, passionate, masculine, feminine

Palmistry Identification

Fire + Saturn

In the hands, the Lovers archetype is represented by the following combination: short fingers, long palm, Fire, and long middle finger, Saturn. Here are hand print examples of the Lovers archetype:

Lovers Hand Print Example 1

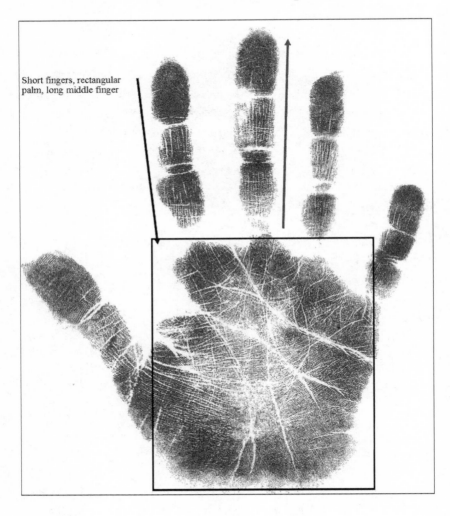

Short fingers, rectangular palm, long middle finger

Lovers Hand Print Example 2

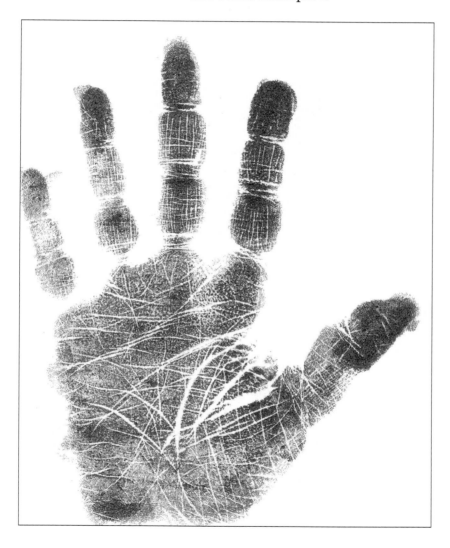

Examples and Exercises

Mudra

To connect with the Lovers in a mudra, interlock your middle, ring and little fingers together while forming a heart shape with your index fingers and thumbs.

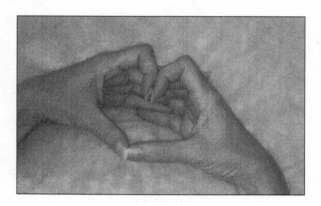

Questions for Growth and Coaches Tips

1. How can I balance my masculine and feminine sides? Look at what defines a masculine trait and a feminine trait. Everyone has many of both. Analyze what is dominant in yourself and what may be dormant or underdeveloped. For example, many people focus much of their time engaging in activities, but don't spend any time meditating or looking inward. This represents an imbalance of too much masculine, or too little feminine. Look at all the competition in the world. Do you see the world this way? If you refocused your attention on cooperation, how would that change things?

2. What do I love to express? This question is to get you thinking about what gets you fired up and excited. Think about what you spend the majority of your time talking

about with others. I get excited about hands and this topic invariably comes up everywhere I go.

3. What can I do to feel sexier? When you feel and express your sexiness, you feel more confident and passionate. Last year I cleared out my entire wardrobe with this focus. If I didn't feel sexy in a particular outfit, I gave it away to charity. I also purchase new items based upon how sexy I feel in them. This also helps you stay young.

4. How can I be more loving to others? Returning ourselves to love is part of our soul's pathway. Listening and being present are two ways that make a huge difference. Have you noticed how technology has created a disconnect in communication? We may be more connected than ever, but what about with the person in front of you? If you're busy checking your phone every two minutes, this is not being present or loving.

5. How can I be more loving to myself? Look for ways that you "prostitute" yourself and decide to change them. For example, do you have a tendency to keep quiet when someone steps in front of you in line, or do you speak up and gently correct the situation? Be in integrity with yourself, you are just as important as everyone else, but be tactful rather than pushy.

Truth Statements for the Lovers

1. My life is balanced through love.
2. I joyfully express my loving nature.
3. I am a loving, sexual being of light.
4. I take time to connect with my sexuality.
5. I integrate opposing energy to become whole.

Chakra Association

Sacral, Heart

Identifying Imbalances

Too much Lovers is represented by prostitution, selling your sexuality for something less than through the pure expression of love. Prostitution can also show up as not being true to yourself and doing something that goes against that. For example, showing up in a church every week that you no longer believe in is a form of prostitution. Too little Lovers is represented by the virgin, not allowing union to occur at all. Virginity may also show up as lack of expression or development in either your sacred masculine or sacred feminine side.

The Lovers at Home

The Lovers at home is a beautiful balance of masculine and feminine elements. Think strong colors combined with lacy curtains in a sitting area or garage tools combined with garden gnomes. The home is obviously occupied by a couple who share everything in harmony.

The Lovers at Work

This archetype is an integration of discipline and creativity. At work, he or she is willing to put in the hours required to get the job done, but also willing to express individuality. Work is productive and original.

The Lovers in Relationships

The Lovers prefer to be in a relationship. This archetype is all about co-existing in harmony with your opposite. It is the combination of traits that make them stronger together than apart. The Lovers enjoy each other, love each other, and celebrate differences.

Best Compatibility

Empress, Strength, Temperance, Sun, World

Good Compatibility

Hierophant, Chariot, Hanged Man, Tower

Challenging Compatibility

High Priestess, Hermit, Death, Judgement, Star, Moon

Opposite Archetype

High Priestess

Famous Lovers Archetypes

Chris Pine, George Clooney, Pepé le Pew

Chapter 7

7–The Chariot

"Progress always involves risks; you can't steal second base and keep your foot on first." — Frederick B. Wilcox

LITTLE THINGS ADD UP TO BIG THINGS. LET ME
share my Chariot story. I am an avid skier, but used to be lazy
in the summer, compromising my workouts. When November
rolled around, I would have a really hard time during my first
few days on skis. I would get winded quickly, and very sore the
next day. I was basically miserable for several weeks, until my
body adjusted again to the physical activity. I finally got fed up
with this reaction, so the next summer I decided I would try to
stay in shape in order to shift my first days of skiing out of pain.

I didn't even do that much, but added little things into my
summer regimen, such as parking further away in a parking lot
or walking up the stairs instead of taking the elevator. By the
next November, my fitness level on the mountain was greatly
improved. I had more energy, more wind and more fun. Was it a
major change in my life that was required? No. It was persistent
action taken over a few months. Even I could hardly believe the
difference it made.

Physical Attributes

From the Lovers, the Chariot brings us back to a single individual, a man standing in his chariot with a black and a white
sphinx, representing a balance of mental and emotional forces,
pulling him onward. He is not holding any reins, but is obviously in full command of his vehicle. Physically, he is strong,
athletic and in control of his direction. Wear clothes that get
you moving to tap into your Chariot, such as workout clothes
or running shoes.

Emotional Attributes

The Chariot is the hero inside us. Emotionally brave and
willing to push through any obstacle, others look up to him.
How would you feel inside if you knew you could not fail? This
is Chariot emotion.

Mental Attributes

Mentally, the Chariot is ambitious. This is a card of movement combined with direction. The mental theme is focused on action and what's next. He is a natural leader. Think about who you look up to and why. What makes that person a good leader? Being able to delegate is an important aspect of leadership. From the card, you can see that the Chariot is not the one "pedaling" the vehicle.

Spiritual Attributes

Spiritually, the Chariot is not comfortable with slow-moving or outdated beliefs. He is always looking at growth including spiritual growth. He is full speed ahead in his development. He naturally looks to improve himself and his position in life. He sets high standards for himself and others.

Key Words for the Chariot

Action, movement, leadership, driven, balanced, determined

Palmistry Identification

Fire + Jupiter

In the hands, the Chariot is represented by the following combination: short fingers, long palm, Fire, and long index finger, Jupiter. Here are hand print examples of the Chariot archetype:

Chariot Hand Print Example 1

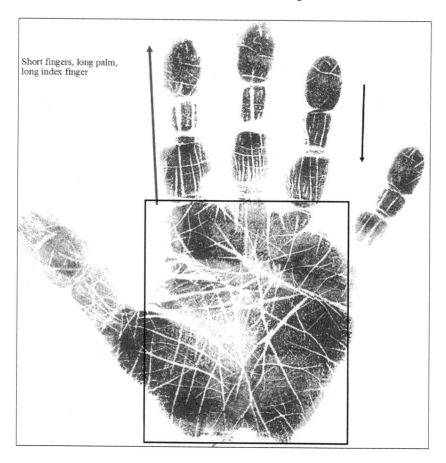

Short fingers, long palm, long index finger

Chariot Hand Print Example 2

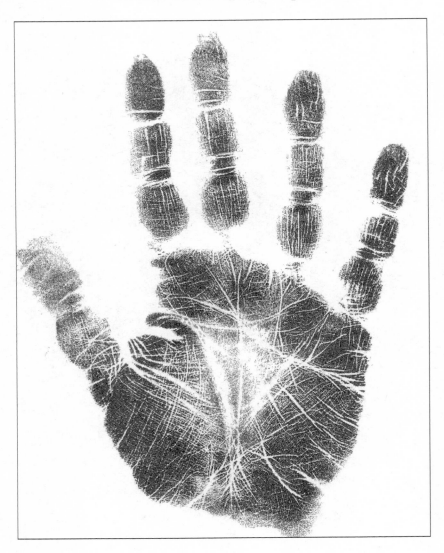

Examples and Exercises

Mudra

To connect to the Chariot in a mudra, place your open hands face down with the index fingers touching at the tips and the thumbs crossed over each other and touching the lower knuckle of each index finger.

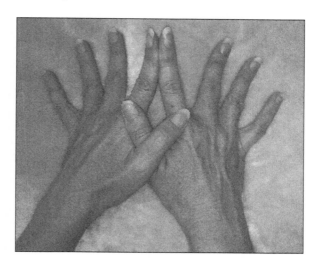

Questions for Growth and Coaches Tips

1. Where in my life have I been procrastinating? This question will help you to see where your hang-ups might be, or where you may have a mental or emotional block.
2. What is the next step I can take right now? It's all about measurable baby steps. Even writing down the next step can help to shift the energy and give you clarity. If you look too far down the road too soon, you might stay immobile.
3. Where do I see myself three months from now, next year and the next five years? Always start with short term views and work up to longer views; energy needs to build

on itself. If you can't see that far out, it's ok. Tap into how you want to feel at that time. For instance, would you like to find your soul mate in the next year? What would he or she feel like in your arms? Bring that feeling into the present.

4. In what ways do other people look up to me? Everyone has natural abilities that other people find attractive. What are yours? What do you find easy to do?

5. How can I expand my vision? For this question, I recommend climbing a mountain, going to the top of a building, or driving to a viewpoint that looks down on a landscape. From this vantage point, ask this question again to yourself. If you can't physically go, visualize a similar place.

Truth Statements for the Chariot

1. I am making progress in my life every day.
2. I am continuously expanding my vision and clarity of direction.
3. My life flows with ease and grace.
4. I easily release stagnation and procrastination.
5. I inspire others through my actions.

Chakra Association

Solar Plexus

Identifying Imbalances

Too much Chariot can result in blind tunnel vision, charging ahead without evaluation along the way. Too little Chariot is stillness and procrastination, being stuck in a rut. Both of these imbalances are rooted in mental and/or emotional blocks.

The Chariot at Home

The Chariot has two fast cars, a snowmobile, wave runners, a speedboat, and an RV in his driveway. He loves to be in motion so his home reflects this. He has a state-of-the-art workout room with all the modern equipment to stay in shape. When he's home, he's working out, but he doesn't spend much time at home. He eats healthy food most of the time, but also enjoys what tastes good. He loves to spend active time in nature. Depending on the season, he's either hiking, biking, skiing or perhaps competing in a triathlon. He doesn't have time for or interest in sitting around. He's never bored.

The Chariot at Work

At work, the Chariot is all about productivity. He gets things done as quickly as possible and doesn't worry about perfection. He makes mistakes, but is harder on himself than anyone else would ever be. People recognize his talents and naturally put him in charge. He's often frustrated by other people's inaction or laziness, leaving them lost sometimes in the dust, or left behind.

The Chariot in Relationships

The Chariot doesn't have time for relationships that drag him down. He is not comfortable with his emotions, particularly when things are not going well. He needs a partner who allows him lots of freedom to do the things he enjoys. If she can keep up, he enjoys active pursuits with her as well. He is a passionate lover, always full of energy and vitality. He is fun to be around, especially when he's winning in other areas of his life. For those who don't understand him, he may come across as superior or competitive.

Best Compatibility

Magician, Emperor, Devil, Judgement

Good Compatibility

Strength, Tower, Sun, World

Challenging Compatibility

Fool, Hermit, Wheel of Fortune, Hanged Man, Moon

Opposite Archetype

Fool

Famous Chariot Archetypes

Jennifer Aniston, Megan Fox, Madonna, Sathya Sai Baba, Harry Potter

Chapter 8

8–Strength

*"You can make your life whatever you
want it to be."* — Wally Amos

MY CONNECTION TO STRENGTH CAME ABOUT when I first transitioned into reading hands professionally. I was lucky enough to meet this kind-hearted man who owned a natural health store. Gifted in his own right, he was an expert in homeopathy and herbs designed to assist his clients in reaching their optimal health. I was introduced to him through a mutual acquaintance. When I first walked into his office, I was not confident that he would be impressed with my work. At the time my client base was under 200, and even though I read to consistently great reviews, I was still just beginning my career. I was also aware that hand analysis was (and still is) considered "pseudo-science" by the uneducated and closed minded.

Not only did this gentleman welcome me into one store to do my readings, but because he had two locations, I worked in two stores. His gentle support let me grow at my own pace, develop my own style, and build my own confidence over time. This was a period of great expansion for me, personally and professionally.

Physical Attributes

This card depicts a woman in a white dress petting a docile lion. Physically, she is obviously not stronger than the lion, but is able to tame it through her kind actions. She is strong and passive at the same time. Wearing soft colors such as pastels and neutral tones can connect you with Strength. Performing static exercises and standing meditation also reflect this archetype.

Emotional Attributes

The Strength archetype is not about emotional domination, but rather showing kindness to achieve goals. Essentially, it's about treating others in a way that you would like to be treated.

Mental Attributes

Mentally, Strength is alert and full of ideas. She is also focused on knowing herself. This is evident from the infinity symbol located above her head. She is very intelligent.

Spiritual Attributes

Strength is spiritually expansive with a focus on love. The infinity symbol also indicates her curiosity and willingness to connect with divine love.

Key Words for Strength

Loving kindness, curiosity, ideas, truth seeking, passive strength, self-aware

Palmistry Identification

Air + Jupiter

In the hands, the Strength archetype is represented by the following combination: long fingers, square palm, Air, and long index finger, Jupiter. Here are hand print examples of the Strength archetype:

Strength Hand Print Example 1

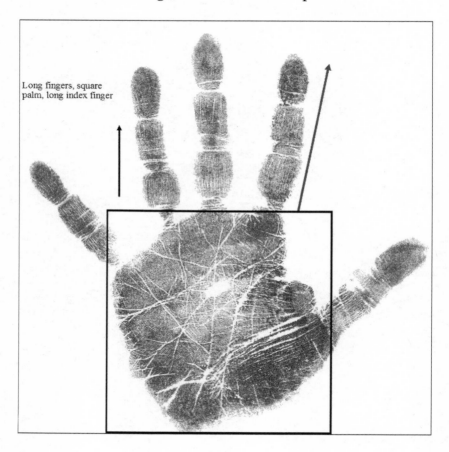

Long fingers, square
palm, long index finger

Strength Hand Print Example 2

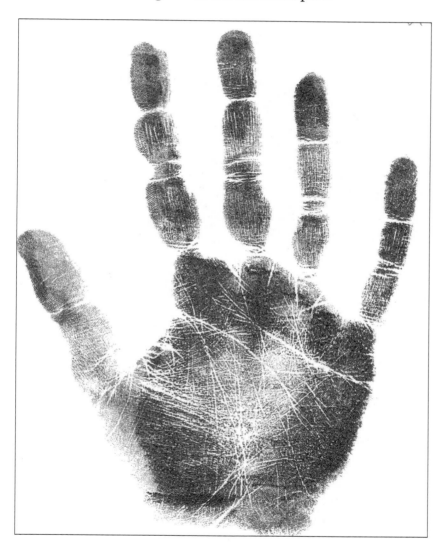

Examples & Exercises

Mudra

To connect with the Strength archetype, place the index finger on the mount just below the little finger on the opposite palm. Then do the same for the opposite hand.

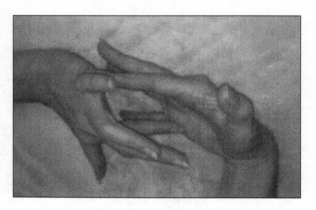

Questions for Growth and Coaches Tips

1. What are my strengths? Focus on your natural strengths to answer this question, the ones you've carried since childhood.
2. How can I surrender more joyfully in my life? Look at areas where you are forcing things or seem to be fighting an uphill battle.
3. How can I get to know myself even better? A fun exercise here is to have a conversation with yourself in a mirror. Talk to yourself as if you're just meeting you for the first the time. You could also do this in a video and play it back to yourself.
4. What big ideas do I have? If barriers were eliminated, what is possible for you?

5. In what ways can I be kinder? A great way to answer this question is to spend time around a loving animal, perhaps a pet dog or a cat. Spend a day at a shelter or borrow your neighbor's pet if you don't have one yourself. Animals teach us unconditional love.

Truth Statements for Strength

1. I am strong regardless of external circumstances.
2. I pursue greater awareness of my strengths.
3. I surrender appropriately to universal consciousness to allow even greater things into my life.
4. I let go of any need to dominate my situation.
5. I choose loving kindness as my path today.

Chakra Association

Heart, Third Eye

Identifying Imbalances

Too much Strength results in achievement through domination, forcing your agenda without thought of consequences or who may get hurt in the process. Too little Strength is having a vision, but because of weakness and ineffectiveness it never comes to pass. It may also show up as lack of self-awareness.

Strength at Home

The Strength archetype is a cooperative housekeeper. She loves to have company over and makes a gracious hostess. She loves to exchange ideas and brainstorm with like-minded people. As a mother, she sets a good example for her children and gives them support and encouragement.

Strength at Work

At work, Strength enjoys the flow of information and being in the loop. She is comfortable in non-profit situations, helping those in need, and innovative in her solutions. She works better with a team that helps facilitate her initiatives, and she naturally takes the lead.

Strength in Relationships

Strength is a loving and considerate partner. She is honest with her feelings and expects her partner to be the same. She is idealistic, and can sometimes be disappointed and disillusioned when things don't work out as planned.

Best Compatibility

Fool, Lovers, Hierophant, Tower, Star

Good Compatibility

High Priestess, Emperor, Wheel of Fortune, Hanged Man, Temperance

Challenging Compatibility

Empress, Sun, Judgement

Opposite Archetype

Sun

Famous Strength Archetypes

Robert DeNiro, Al Pacino, John F. Kennedy, Cynthia Nixon, the Dalai Lama, Hillary Clinton, Lady Gaga, Mary Poppins

Chapter 9

9–The Hermit

"The larger the island of knowledge, the longer the
shoreline of wonder." — Ralph W. Sockman

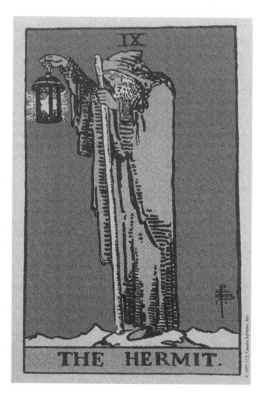

THINKING BACK TO SOME OF THE GREAT INFLU-
encers in my life, one of my Hermit connections came from my
French teacher, Madame Falsone. I studied French under her
for three years in junior high school. Choosing to study another
language is a very personal and inward decision. I suspect I've
had many past lives in France, and perhaps this was part of my
subconscious longing to reconnect. At the time, my teenage self
chose to study French because I felt it was a beautiful language
and I wanted to absorb that beauty. In my mind it was more
beautiful than Spanish or German, although now I find that
every language has its own splendor and personality. Madame
Falsone taught me the basics of the language – pronunciation,
writing, proper spelling and grammar – and also the essence of
the language, from a culture of people who enjoy living life to the
fullest. Under her gentle tutelage, I discovered French food, po-
etry and lifestyle. French came alive when she introduced us to
the qualities of its soul. *Joie de vivre* was no longer an abstract
concept, but a sensation running through my core.

Physical Attributes

This card depicts an elderly man in gray robes holding a
walking stick and a shining lantern. He looks like a kind grand-
parent. The Hermit may remind you of the Hierophant, and yes,
they are cousins. But the Hermit's pathway is more personal
than universal, drawing on his own intuition rather than the
traditions of others. He is alone in the card, having climbed the
mountain in search of enlightenment for himself. For you to
be in touch with the Hermit, take some time and contemplate
your outfit for the day. Choose colors that align with what you're
trying to achieve that day. For example, to be more fluid, wear
blue or black. To be joyful, wear yellow or bright pink. To be
passionate, wear red. To be pure, wear white.

Emotional Attributes

Emotionally, the Hermit feels inwardly. He processes his emotions by himself. He takes full responsibility for his life, sometimes releasing others of burdens that may be easier to share. He prefers to figure things out on his own before going to someone else. In order to be in harmony with this archetype, pause before reacting. Be patient and kind.

Mental Attributes

Mentally, the Hermit is contemplative. He knows much, but says little, unless asked by a truly interested person. Outwardly he may appear clueless, but inwardly he is sharp and intelligent. If you are lucky enough to get him to talk, listen attentively, because there is great wisdom to be shared. Ask him philosophical questions and listen carefully. To mentally engage your inner Hermit, find something new to read or learn that increases your wisdom.

Spiritual Attributes

The Hermit is interested in spiritual growth. He is seeking wholeness within himself through the lonely pathway of self-development and enlightenment. Become a seeker of truth from many sources to connect deeply with the Hermit.

Key Words for the Hermit

Wisdom, truth, inner guidance, independent, teacher, reflective, contemplative, smart

Palmistry Identification

Earth + Mercury

In the hands, the Hermit archetype is represented by the following combination: short fingers, square palm, Earth, and long little finger, Mercury. Here are hand print examples of the Hermit archetype:

The Hermit Hand Print Example 1

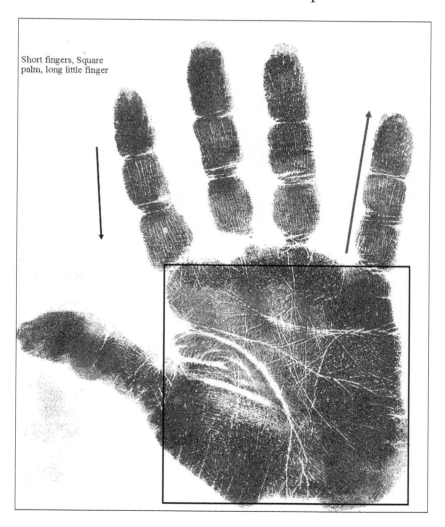

Short fingers, Square
palm, long little finger

Hermit Hand Print Example 2

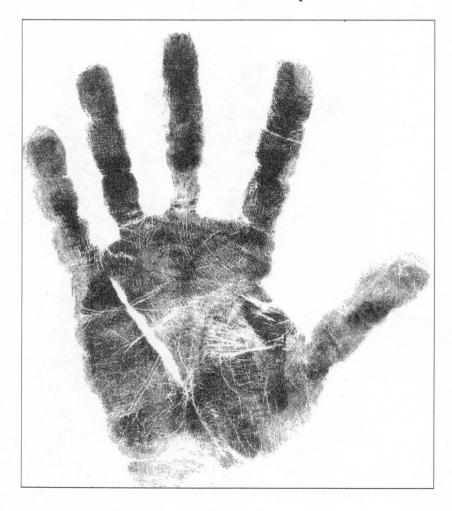

Examples and Exercises

Mudra

To connect to the Hermit archetype in a mudra, interlock all the fingers and thumbs of both hands inwardly to each other.

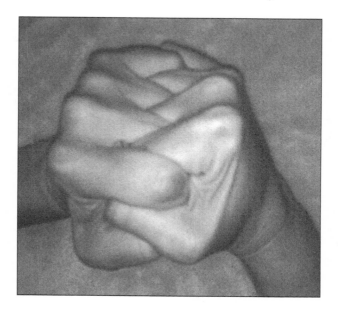

Questions for Growth and Coaches Tips

1. What would I like to learn more about? Make a list of things you're interested in. Now when you look at this list, prioritize them. Give yourself permission to be a student again; go to the library and find some books on the subject. Take time to read every week instead of watching TV.

2. How can I enhance my connection with my spiritual self? To grow in this archetype, you must commit to spending time alone. When you are in your own energy, it is easier to connect with your spiritual side. Take a

quick assessment of how much time you actually spend in a week by yourself. I recommend creating a special sanctuary spot just for meditation, reading and contemplation. Put a sign on your door if you have to and communicate with your loved ones.

3. Do I get enough time to myself? If not, what can I do by myself today? If you are currently spending less than seven hours alone in a week, something needs to shift. Being in your car doesn't count, since you are actively engaged with other drivers and road conditions.

4. How can I increase my meditation time? Meditation sometimes seems like a four letter word. I've spoken with countless people about how important this is, but there is so much misunderstanding around it. Rather than try to start out with an hour then give up frustrated forevermore, begin with two or three minutes. Practice with the balances I describe in chapter one as good starting points.

5. How can I get into nature more often? Being in nature is one of the best ways to get in touch with the Hermit. A quiet walk among trees, birds and flowers is not only a fantastic way to move your body, but it will clear your head and calm your spirit too. Make a date with nature, just like you would make a date with a girlfriend or a client. Then stick to it, at least once each week. *But it's cold and wintery now*, you may be thinking. All the more reason to get outside. Leave the hibernation to the bears. No excuses!

Truth Statements for the Hermit

1. I choose to keep learning and studying new things.
2. I balance my time alone and my time with others.
3. I enjoy spending time in nature.
4. I take time to meditate.

5. I am whole and complete within myself.

Chakra Association

Root, Third Eye

Identifying Imbalances

Too much Hermit is about becoming a know-it-all and looking down on the ignorance of others. Too little Hermit is spending too much time with others at the expense of learning and growing inwardly.

The Hermit at Home

The Hermit is not concerned with his surroundings in terms of cleanliness or orderliness. He just wants to be warm and comfortable in his home. He cares about having spaces that are just for him, even if he shares his home with a family.

The Hermit at Work

At work, the Hermit is productive and fully aware of what needs to be done. He is competent and extremely adept in his field of expertise. He knows more than he shares with others unless they need to know it. He pulls knowledge out when and where it's needed, then lets it go when it's not. He works well alone without needing anyone pushing him to be motivated.

The Hermit in Relationships

In relationships, the Hermit can be a hard person to figure out. He is independent, but once in a relationship, he is committed and dedicated. He can also be charming and funny too. He brings a sense of security to his partner along with a bit of mystery. He makes a good parent, strict but fair.

Best Compatibility

High Priestess, Hanged Man, Death

Good Compatibility

Fool, Emperor, Star, Moon, Sun

Challenging Compatibility

Magician, Hierophant, Chariot, Devil, Tower, World

Opposite Archetype

Hierophant

Famous Hermit Archetypes

Prince William, Vladimir Putin, Anthony Robbins, Peyton Manning, Yoda, Hermione Granger, Spock

Chapter 10

10 – Wheel of Fortune

"You're never a loser until you quit trying." — Mike Ditka

HAVE YOU EVER HAD THE FEELING ON WAKING up one morning that you were just going to be lucky that day? That fate was on your side and something wonderful was about to happen, even though you had no idea how it would happen? I remember one of these days when I was on vacation in South Lake Tahoe, Nevada. This is a place with some large casinos and gambling of all types. My former husband was fond of gambling, so I learned to play various games including blackjack. This particular day brought us to a casino that was offering a video blackjack tournament with the first-place prize of $400 for a minimal entry fee. Normally I do not participate in tournaments, but this day I was feeling good about it so I signed up.

There were hundreds of other participants playing in two rounds of competition. I was leading after the first round so I was invited back to the final round that evening. I was delighted when I showed up later and accepted the option to choose the machine I would be competing on. I decided on the same machine I'd played that morning, figuring if it worked for me once, why not again? The competition was abuzz with excitement and I had a very strong second round. After a short wait to determine the winner, I was presented with the first place prize. This was my connection to the Wheel of Fortune.

Physical Attributes

The tarot switches gears on us with the Wheel of Fortune card, in that a person is not central to the card's image. Instead we see a wheel with unusual symbols on it as the center of the card. Surrounding it are various animals and mythical creatures displayed on the wheel or on clouds in the background. To connect to the energy of this card, the Wheel is showing us to flow with life, to smile and believe that things are rolling along as they need to. Dress for success and don't be afraid to be noticed. Act as if what you wish to achieve is inevitable.

Emotional Attributes

The Wheel of Fortune is emotionally supported and knows it. If you are not feeling this in your life, do this first for yourself. Pay attention to how you feel about yourself. Do you feel undeserving, unworthy or unlovable? Change this and know you are completely deserving, worthy and lovable. Then feel it.

Mental Attributes

Mentally, the Wheel of Fortune is untroubled in his mind. He allows fate to take him where he needs to be when he needs to be there. He is open to possibility. Affirm to yourself that you are lucky, that you get your parking space, you are healthy, you trust in things working in your favor, and opportunities abound.

Spiritual Attributes

The Wheel of Fortune believes in luck. He aligns himself spiritually to be able to receive that luck, then moves into positive expectancy that it will happen when the time is right.

Key Words for the Wheel of Fortune

Luck, serendipity, wealth, abundance, flow, opportunity

Palmistry Identification

Fire + Apollo

In the hands, the Wheel of Fortune archetype is represented by the following combination: short fingers, rectangular palm, Fire, and long ring finger. Here are hand print examples of the Wheel of Fortune archetype:

Wheel of Fortune Hand Print Example 1

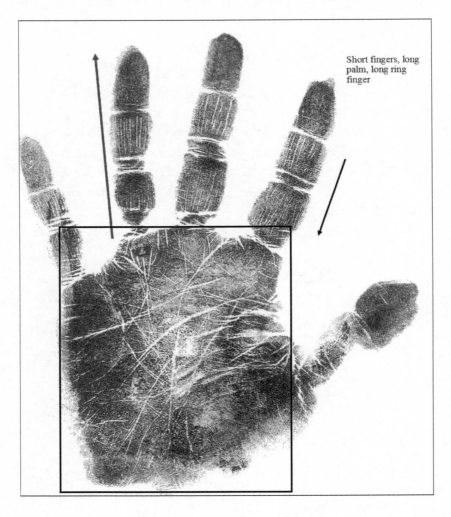

Short fingers, long palm, long ring finger

Wheel of Fortune Hand Print Example 2

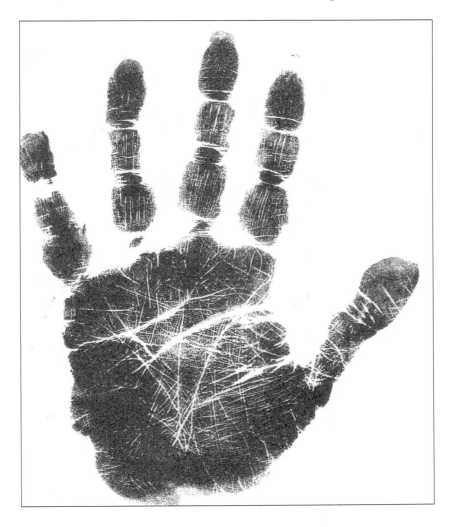

Examples and Exercises

Mudra

To connect to the Wheel of Fortune in a mudra, place open palms facing each other with relaxed and open fingers. Touch the opposite ring fingers together and the thumbs together.

Questions for Growth and Coaches Tips

1. How can I align myself to be more in flow with the universe? Look at what's "flowing" in your life and what is not. Or what is "leaking," which could indicate wasted flow or misdirected flow. A common block people experience is the belief that there needs to be a struggle before something wonderful can happen. This simply is not true. Change your belief to affirm that things flow easily and effortlessly, and you are fully deserving of whatever you desire.

2. What does luck feel like? Go back to a time in your past when you experienced good luck. Use that experience as a vibrational record to tap into that frequency again.

3. How can I feel more supported? The idea behind this question is to help you start building your own "platform." When you feel supported, it's easier to be in flow. Start identifying different areas of your life, such as your home, office, friends and family. Then look at each area and evaluate how it supports you now. What little things can you do to increase support?

4. Who in my life supports me and who does not? If you spend a lot of time around people who squelch your dreams, consider shifting your direction. Spend more time around people who have dreams and visions similar to your own, so you feel more encouraged.

5. How can I share my positive energy with others? Spreading luck is a fun way to play in the world around you. For example, whenever I'm riding in a car with someone and we're heading to a busy place, I affirm that the perfect parking spot is waiting for us. Guess what, it always shows up when I do this!

Truth Statements for the Wheel of Fortune

1. I create luck every day.
2. My life is in alignment with the flow of the universe.
3. I am fully supported in all ways.
4. I choose to be happy even when challenging things happen.
5. I release the need to control specific outcomes in my life.

Chakra Association

Crown

Identifying Imbalances

Too much Wheel of Fortune results in greed and the need to micromanage every part of your life. Too little Wheel of Fortune appears as bad luck and patterns repeating themselves; being out of flow or out of alignment.

The Wheel of Fortune at Home

At home, the Wheel of Fortune is instinctual with décor. He places furnishings and colors in such a way that feels right in the moment, but may change his mind shortly thereafter. His surroundings are comfortable, refined and luxurious. He is not afraid to be a little over the top, installing a bowling alley, perhaps, or huge theater room if it suits him. He happily shares his fortune with those he cares about.

The Wheel of Fortune at Work

At work, he needs to be seen and appreciated for his talents and skills. He prefers to be the center of attention. He learns new skills quickly and delivers efficiently. He also gets bored easily and continuously needs a new challenge or project to stay interested. He's hard to keep up with sometimes because so much changes around him. He thrives on and welcomes change.

The Wheel of Fortune in Relationships

In relationships, the Wheel of Fortune may have trouble finding a partner interesting or energetic enough to keep up with him. He may be a little fickle. But he's also exciting and fun to be around, and there's always something going on. His partner needs to shower him with compliments because inside he may actually be insecure. He values reassurance, and this keeps him going.

Best Compatibility

Magician, Temperance, Moon

Good Compatibility

Fool, Strength, Sun, Judgement

Challenging Compatibility

Emperor, Chariot, Death, Justice, Star

Opposite Archetype

Death

Famous Wheel of Fortune Archetypes

Michael Jackson, Johnny Depp, Angelina Jolie, Robert Downey, Jr., Daniel Radcliffe, Gerald Ford, Martin Luther King, Jr.

Chapter 11

11–Justice

"It's easy to dodge our responsibilities, but we cannot dodge the consequences of dodging our responsibilities." — Sir Josiah Stamp

WHEN I WAS IN ELEMENTARY SCHOOL, THERE was a blind girl in our class. Her name was Cynthia, too, so I felt that I had a connection with her even though we were not actually friends. One day, the entire class was called to an assembly. The faculty addressed some cruel treatment Cynthia had been receiving around her disability. Kids can definitely be mean sometimes, driven by their own insecurities and pressure to fit in with their peers. As a result of that event, everyone in the class was required to take turns being blindfolded and guided by another student. This connection with Justice gave everyone the opportunity to appreciate their eyesight and gain compassion for this girl. The cruelty stopped after this experience. Although I was not one of the kids participating in thoughtless acts, I did find the lesson valuable. It was an innovative way for the teachers to generate Justice and teach an essential lesson to each of us.

Physical Attributes

The Justice card shows a woman in red robes sitting with a sword and scales. She is like our modern-day judge. To be in alignment with Justice, wear clothes that have been made ethically and sustainably, rather than in a low-paying sweatshop type environment.

Emotional Attributes

Emotionally, Justice represents neutrality. Not angry, sad, bitter or fearful. She stays calm and expresses herself without needing to raise her voice. When she's balanced, she doesn't lose her composure by expressing extreme emotions.

Mental Attributes

Mentally, Justice is all about fairness. She understands there are at least two sides or two perspectives for every thought. She works to include them all to bring about harmony.

Spiritual Attributes

Justice is spiritually impartial. She is open to different belief systems and may choose to study them, but ultimately chooses the one that is balanced and makes the most sense to her.

Key Words for Justice

Fair, balanced, impartial, neutral

Palmistry Identification

Water + Saturn

In the hands, the Justice archetype is represented by the following combination: long fingers, rectangular palm, Water, and long middle finger. Here are hand print examples of the Justice archetype:

Justice Hand Print Example 1

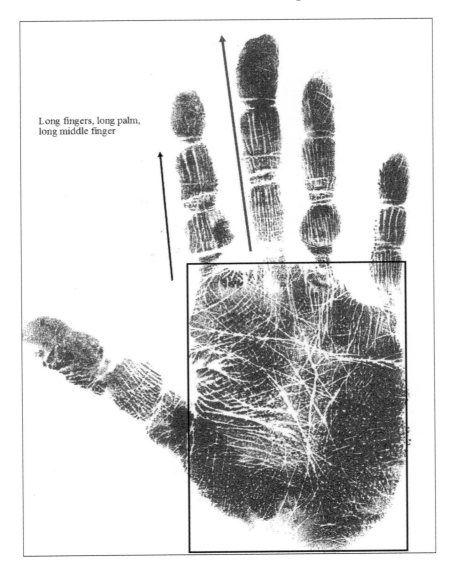

Long fingers, long palm,
long middle finger

Cynthia Clark

Justice Hand Print Example 2

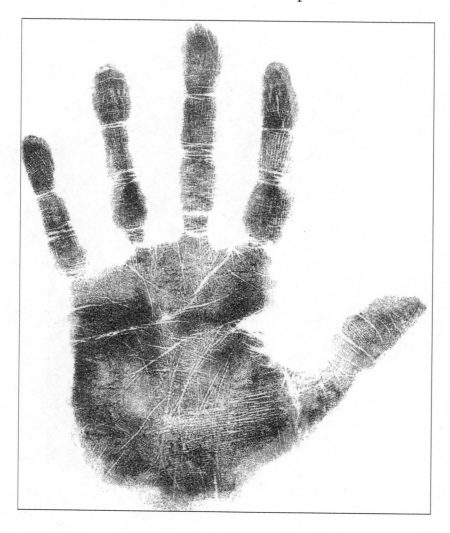

Examples and Exercises

Mudra

To connect to the Justice archetype in a mudra, first place the palms together at the base away from the thumbs (see the picture on the left.) Next, bring the middle fingers together at the fingernails. Place all other fingers and the thumbs in an open position (see the picture on the right.)

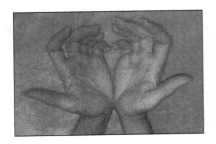 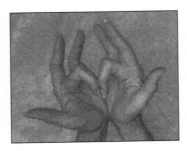

Questions for Growth and Coaches Tips

1. What injustices do I feel strongly about? Answering this question shows you what needs to heal within yourself. When you know and understand that there is a reason behind every "injustice," and you don't have to be the one to fix it or change it, this takes the pressure off you and allows you to refocus your attention more positively. For example, if you feel bitter over an event where someone hurt you in the past, this shows you the area where you can forgive yourself and the other person. Don't underestimate the power of this. Real forgiveness can free you so quickly and completely, while holding on to bitterness can keep you trapped. Don't let this be you! It may be easier to do if you look at the other person from the perspective of the inner child. Take away all the masks and pain to see the divine underneath.

2. What action can I take today to bring in greater neutral-
    ity? If you are "anti" anything, that may serve to bring
    more of that action into the world, because your subcon-
    scious does not recognize negative words. Therefore, if
    your focus is on "anti-war efforts," your subconscious
    translates this into "war efforts," and works to bring
    about more war, the very opposite of the peace you ac-
    tually desire. It's time to take responsibility for your
    thoughts and actions and re-focus your energy on what
    you want to see in the world, not on what you don't want
    to see.

3. What injustice from my past can I let go of now through
    forgiveness? Make a list of people or events that you
    feel were unjust. Even if you don't mean it at first, start
    thinking, "I forgive you." Just speaking the words can
    initiate the healing process. Pay attention to how much
    lighter you feel afterward.

4. What do I feel emotionally charged about? This question
    can help you identify where you place blame in the uni-
    verse. When you take one hundred percent responsibility
    for your life, it takes away the need to blame anyone for
    anything. Ultimately, you are the creator of your world.
    Again, this shows where you can heal yourself, so you are
    no longer a prisoner of external circumstances.

5. How can I get back into emotional neutrality? Make a
    list of positive emotions such as joy, happiness, peace,
    or tranquility. Next to each emotion, ask yourself what
    brings you that. Then, when you find yourself emotion-
    ally charged, do one of the things on your list.

Truth Statements for Justice

1. I create fairness in my life, knowing the universe sup-
    ports me.
2. I dissolve destructive emotions easily and quickly.

3. I believe in universal justice; life is more than fair.
4. I behave in fair and just ways with myself and others.
5. I forgive and release perceived injustices from my past.

Chakra Association

Throat

Identifying Imbalances

Too much Justice becomes the overly judgmental vigilante. Too little Justice results in bitterness without resolution or the ability to forgive.

Justice at Home

At home, Justice makes a great parent. She allows her child to grow and develop, but does not behave as her friend. She offers firm advice and guidance, but also appropriate punishment for misbehavior to help her grow. She is diplomatic in all household decisions.

Justice at Work

At work, Justice is cooperative and serious about her work. She takes her time, and sometimes too much time to accomplish tasks. She benefits from music being played at work to make the day go by more positively. She is deeply moved by the suffering of others, whether it's a coworker or a minority group, and will do anything she can for them.

Justice in Relationships

Justice likes to play fair in relationships; she is not a game player. She expects the same from her partner. Sometimes she gets depressed and needs a boost from her partner. She does well with someone who is able to handle her mood swings without being pulled down himself. Justice likes to have a secure and stable partnership that eventually leads to marriage.

Best Compatibility

Emperor, Hierophant, Judgement

Good Compatibility

Empress, Death, Temperance, Moon, Sun

Challenging Compatibility

Magician, Wheel of Fortune, Hanged Man, Devil, Tower, Star

Opposite Archetype

Magician

Famous Justice Archetypes

Keira Knightly, Britney Spears, Batman

Chapter 12

12–Hanged Man

"Life is not about waiting for the storms to pass...it's about learning how to dance in the rain." — Vivian Greene

SOMETIMES WE MAY FEEL LIKE LIFE IS UNFAIR
and we're being punished by the universe. It's true that being
here on earth is full of challenges. But if we just look at things
a different way, we can find that it's all in our best interest after all. The universe is actually conspiring in our favor. I had
a connection with the Hanged Man during a break up period
with my boyfriend. At the time I was devastated that this could
possibly happen, but that period of independence taught me
more about myself, and gave me the opportunity to really know
and understand my own value. This "giving up" allowed me to
reset in areas of my life that would not have been possible if we
had just stayed together. I learned about my own strength, my
resiliency, my freedom, and my resolve, among other things.
Being far enough past it and looking back, I now realize that all
our challenges are actually opportunities for our own spiritual
growth.

Physical Attributes

Sometimes a misunderstood card, at first glance you might
think of the Hanged Man as doom and gloom, such as going to
the gallows. *Oh no, how did he get like that?* But a closer look at
him reflects someone who seems quite content after all. The illumination around his head is showing us that he is choosing to
be upside down, hanging from his foot. His outfit includes blue,
representing emotions, and red, representing desires. These
are being stilled for a period of reconsideration. For you to understand the Hanged Man, try inverting yourself. This is done
in yoga classes all the time. Do a hand stand or a head stand,
or even just get on a couch and hang your head over the edge.

Emotional Attributes

Emotionally, the Hanged Man is surrendering. He is allowing himself to feel a different way than what may be expected

or approved. He is following his own emotional flow, wherever that may lead. Allow yourself to tune into your own feelings, don't push them away or make them wrong.

Mental Attributes

Mentally, the Hanged Man is looking at different points of view. Being upside down, he is showing us that our perspective can change our reality. He is naturally innovative, curious and open minded. Look at viewpoints that you hold and ask yourself what a broader viewpoint might look like.

Spiritual Attributes

Spiritually, the Hanged Man is accepting of his path, but chooses to look at it from another angle in order to move through it. By recognizing the illusions of a fixed perspective, he is free to choose his own course toward spiritual enlightenment.

Key Words for the Hanged Man

Giving up, surrendering, new perspective, innovative

Palmistry Identification

Water + Fire

For the first time, we have an archetype that is not determined by a strong finger. Instead, we have a combination of two elements, water and fire. These elements are opposites, yet can and do exist in some people's hands. This can show up in two ways. Either the person has a water hand with fire lines or a fire hand with water lines. The second combination shows up more often, as you will see below. Here are hand print examples of the Hanged Man archetype:

Hanged Man Hand Print Example 1

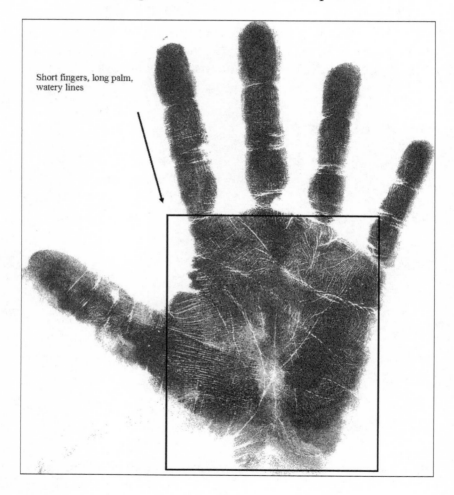

Short fingers, long palm, watery lines

Hanged Man Hand Print Example 2

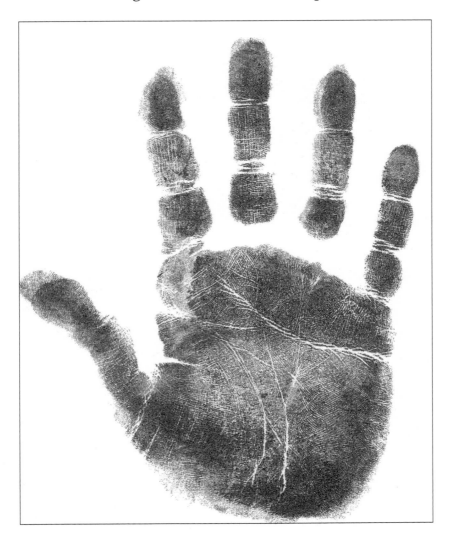

Examples and Exercises

Mudra

To connect to the Hanged Man in a mudra, interlock all of your fingers except the thumbs, with the fingers pointing down.

Questions for Growth and Coaches Tips

1. How can I look at my situation from a different perspective? Begin to look at everything as an opportunity, especially the challenges in your life. For example, in the last two years, I have had to move quite a bit. I could look at this as a pain in the butt, as many people do. Instead, I have chosen to look at it as an opportunity to let go of belongings I don't need and continually open myself to new experiences. It is necessary to surrender a limiting belief to make room for a new belief that supports your goals.

2. What if the opposite were true? Let's say you just lost your business partner. You might be thinking, *now I'm screwed*. But with his energy out of the way, you end up meeting a new partner better suited to work with you, and together you take the business to a place that brings you more joy and success.

3. In what ways am I being rigid in my thinking? Take a look at your "always" and "never" statements. These

words restrict and confine. For example, do you always get sick during "flu" season? What if you stopped focusing on the belief that there even IS a flu season? How would your life change if you started to believe that all seasons are healthy seasons? I can tell you this single switch can and will improve your health. Don't buy into fear-based blanket beliefs.

4. What can I do differently? This question gets you in the driver seat. As Gandhi said, you must be the change you wish to see in the world. You have the power to change your beliefs and your actions to be in alignment with your desires. What you focus on expands.

5. What needs to change to create a new outcome? Make a list of your current outcomes. For example, look at your bank balances, your weight, your significant relationships, your work satisfaction. If your bank balance is less than you'd like it to be, you need to change your relationship with money. If you're in a lousy romantic relationship, you need to change your relationship with yourself. Your inner world reflects your outer world. Change the inner world and your outer world will catch up and reflect it. Just remember to be consistent, since there can be a lag time before experiencing the result.

Truth Statements for the Hanged Man

1. I am able and willing to look at things differently.
2. I surrender rigid beliefs to be realigned.
3. I am able to change my perspective.
4. My life is full of infinite possibilities.
5. I look at things with love and humor.

Chakra Association

Solar Plexus, Third Eye

Identifying Imbalances

Too much Hanged Man is the rebel just to be the rbel, without any real reason. Too little Hanged Man is being stuck in rigid and fixed perspectives.

The Hanged Man at Home

The Hanged Man at home has an unusual dwelling, typically non-traditional, but fun and comfortable. He keeps his own schedule and has a variety of foods in his fridge. He makes good company and enjoys sharing his passionate ways with others.

The Hanged Man at Work

At work, the Hanged Man definitely gets noticed. This may be good or bad depending on his profession. He comes up with unusual solutions and challenges authority, especially if it doesn't make sense to him.

The Hanged Man in Relationships

In relationships, the Hanged Man is fun, exciting and in touch with his emotional side, although he may get caught up in drama if he's not careful. He can also be moody or simply indecisive. If you want to have a successful relationship with him, it's important to be able to go with the flow and avoid making rigid plans too far in advance. For example, it's great to plan a vacation, but don't plan every activity for every day. Allow for some flexibility and spontaneity.

Best Compatibility

Hermit, Death, Tower, Moon

Good Compatibility

Magician, Lovers, Strength, Devil

Challenging Compatibility

Hierophant, Chariot, Justice

Opposite Archetype

None, the Hanged Man integrates the opposing elements of fire and water

Famous Hanged Man Archetypes

Johnny Depp, George W. Bush, Greta Garbo, Mark Twain, Jimmy Carter, JK Rowling

Chapter 13

13–Death

"When patterns are broken, new worlds emerge." — Tuli Kupferberg

WHEN I WAS A CHILD IN ELEMENTARY SCHOOL I had asthma, which restricted me from doing vigorous exercise. I believe we have illnesses for a reason and I think I had some subconscious feelings of fear and unworthiness when I was young. When I was eleven, my brother introduced me to a game called hacky sack. This game involves kicking a small, squishy ball filled with beads. I was entranced by the simple elegance of it, and liked the fact that I could play it by myself, since I had no interest in competitive sports. Hacky sack can be quite aerobic when you get good at it, so my asthma posed a problem. But I was determined and practiced every day to the best of my ability.

What I noticed was that as my skill improved, my asthma went away. By the time I was twelve, my illness was completely gone, and though my lung capacity isn't as strong as it might be, I've never had this problem again. This was my first experience with Death. I attribute my "cure" to being mindful about choosing to do something I enjoyed and letting go of negative feelings through exercise. As I became more skilled, I let go of fear and felt more worthy. It was a transformation of consciousness.

Physical Attributes

Another commonly misunderstood card, Death in tarot very rarely indicates physical death. This is not a card to fear. In the card, we see a skeletal figure dressed in armor and sitting on horseback carrying a black flag with a white flower. This image reminds us of the Four Horsemen of the Apocalypse. There is also a religious figure in yellow who appears to be praying. In the background we see a sunrise. Physically, Death represents impermanence and changeability. A more positive name for this card is the butterfly. To become something new, the caterpillar must transform. To connect to Death "shed your skin," change your clothes, get a haircut or buy a new ring.

Emotional Attributes

Emotionally, Death is about letting go and releasing unwanted emotions. It is through releasing that more positive emotions can arise. Crying is a great way to release emotional energy. Tears flowing can be quite healing. If you ever feel like you need to cry, don't view this as a weakness in yourself. It is your body's way of opening and releasing. Yelling is another way to release, but this technique is better done into a pillow or somewhere you won't disturb others.

Mental Attributes

Mentally, Death is about recognizing the darkness within, the shadow side, analyzing what's not working anymore. Analyze any illness you may have as a pathway to change.

Spiritual Attributes

Spiritually, the Death archetype is all about transformation. Think of the mythical bird, the phoenix, who rises out of the ashes to fly free once more. It is through seeing and experiencing darkness that leads us back to the light. Ultimately, all experiences are for your benefit, to help you grow and transform, even if you don't see them that way at first.

Key Words for Death

Endings, beginnings, releasing, shedding, transformation

Palmistry Identification

Water + Jupiter

In the hands, the Death archetype is represented by the following combination: long fingers, rectangular palm, Water, and long index finger, Jupiter. Here are hand print examples of the Death archetype:

Death Hand Print Example 1

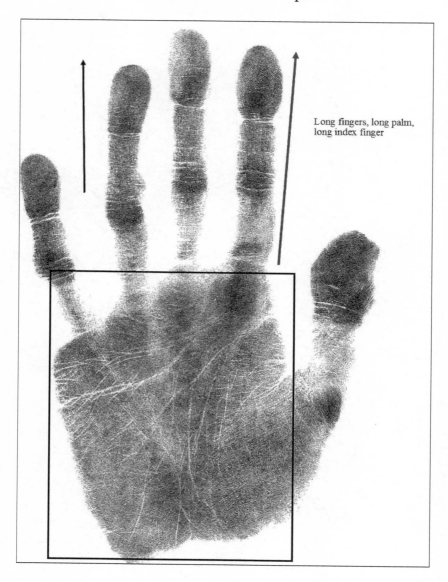

Long fingers, long palm, long index finger

Death Hand Print Example 2

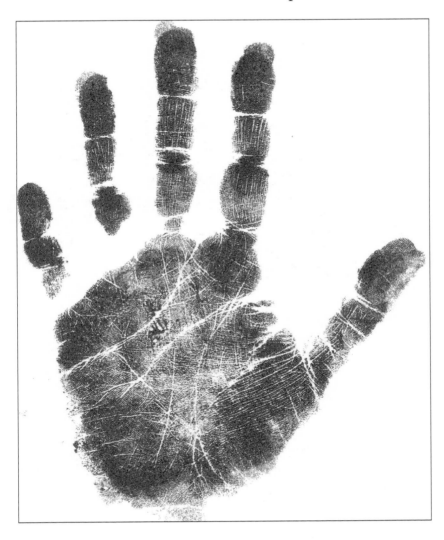

Examples and Exercises

Mudra

To connect to the Death archetype in a mudra, with palms up, place the thumbs inside each palm, positioning them just below the mount under the little finger (see photo on the left.) This is known as the Pluto mount. Next close all the fingers over the thumbs (see photo on the right.)

 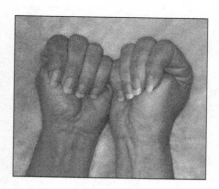

Questions for Growth and Coaches Tips

1. What can I let go of that I don't need anymore? This may include a physical illness, a tangible item, an outdated belief, a temperament or a person in your life.
2. What wants to be reborn inside me? If you didn't have any restrictions holding you back, who would you be, how would you feel, what greatness would emerge from you? The problem with most people is that they automatically discount a possibility since it hasn't come true for them yet. Just because it hasn't come to pass doesn't mean that it can't or won't.
3. What emotions am I holding onto that are toxic? Many people run emotional patterning over and over, day after day. This question can help you identify patterns in

you that need to be released. Focus around your "pain" points: what causes you pain and angst? These are areas of unresolved feelings inside you.

4. What can I change within me or around me to create a more positive existence? Look at opportunities for freshening things up. This can be as simple as getting rid of an old couch or throwing away papers or magazines you haven't looked at in a long time. Maybe you have a mole or wart on your body; why not get it removed?

5. Where do I feel stagnant in my life? Maybe a relationship needs to shift, or you need a change of location. When was the last time you took a trip out of state or country? Try taking a different route home from work or adjusting your attitude about other drivers. Stagnation can appear in all sorts of ways. Be honest with yourself and reexamine your routines.

Truth Statements for Death

1. I am able and willing to let go of old destructive patterns.
2. I choose to let go of stagnation and embrace change.
3. I am transforming my life in positive ways.
4. My life and body are renewing all the time.
5. I recognize and bless my challenges.

Chakra Association

Crown

Identifying Imbalances

Too much Death is pushing away things that could alter your life in a positive way and continuing to choose destructive or stagnant pathways. This could include killing the "good" in your life or ending things too soon. Too little Death is holding on to what no longer serves, being trapped in the dark night of the soul, fearing change and procrastinating.

Death at Home

At home, Death surrounds herself with transformational tools. She may have a place for meditation or a place to cry. She enjoys dark rooms as much as bright rooms, but clearly likes to be in charge of her surroundings. She intuitively knows where things belong and she's not afraid to throw things out.

Death at Work

At work, Death is demanding and can come across as bossy, but her authoritarianism is for everyone's benefit. She is good at seeing what needs to be done and is not afraid to speak her mind. Her high standards improve everyone's work. She makes a good team leader as long as she deals with her own insecurities first.

Death in Relationships

In relationships, Death is idealistic and expects a lot from her partner. Her emotional intensity can be too much for some men. She needs a strong and stable man who can keep her satisfied, both physically and emotionally. She is searching for a deep soul connection with a partner who appreciates her gifts and is willing to transform and improve himself.

Best Compatibility

High Priestess, Hermit, Hanged Man, Devil

Good Compatibility

Empress, Star, Moon, Judgement

Challenging Compatibility

Magician, Lovers, Wheel of Fortune, World

Opposite Archetype

Wheel of Fortune

Famous Death Archetypes

Liv Tyler, Princess Diana, Queen of Hearts

Chapter 14

14–Temperance

"The best way out is always through." — Robert Frost

I WAS FORCED TO CONNECT WITH TEMPERANCE
during the time that I broke my hand in karate class. I had to
wear a cast for four weeks and couldn't get it wet. Luckily it was
my passive hand, but I was amazed to discover how much we
use both of our hands all the time. This becomes so obvious
when one of them suddenly doesn't work anymore. You know
what the worst part of that experience was? I had a hard time
pulling up my pants. I couldn't wear anything other than sweats
because there was no way to manage a zipper. I'm certainly not
part of the fashion police, but when the cast finally came off
I was so grateful to be able to wear my favorite jeans again. I
remember reveling for weeks afterward about how remarkable
it was to have two working hands. I would often look at them
and say "Thank you hands for being with me!" Sometimes an
accident or illness forces us to adjust to a new way of being for
a period of time. This period gave me a new appreciation of my
body and all of its functions.

Physical Attributes

The Temperance card shows us an angel in white standing
with one foot in the water and the other on the shore, while
transferring water from one goblet to another. His white robe
is adorned with a triangle. There is balance here being shown
in multiple ways. Physically, to connect with Temperance, wear
clothes that are modest and blend in with your surroundings.
Look people in the eye, but don't stare. Speak clearly, but not
too loudly or too quietly.

Emotional Attributes

Emotionally, Temperance is stable, not getting too excited
or too down. He adjusts his emotions to diffuse any charged
situations.

Mental Attributes

Mentally, Temperance takes a diplomatic stance, not too controversial, and uses sound reasoning to work through differences. He is "the voice of reason" who helps everyone get back on track. Whenever you are faced with difficulties, ask yourself "what is a reasonable approach?"

Spiritual Attributes

Temperance is spiritually evolved to balance what works. The triangle represents alignment with emotional, mental and spiritual aspects of the self.

Key Words for Temperance

Balanced, stable, adjusting, artistic

Palmistry Identification

Air + Apollo

In the hands, the Temperance archetype is represented by the following combination: long fingers, square palm, Air, and long ring finger, Apollo. Here are hand print examples of the Temperance archetype:

Temperance Hand Print Example 1

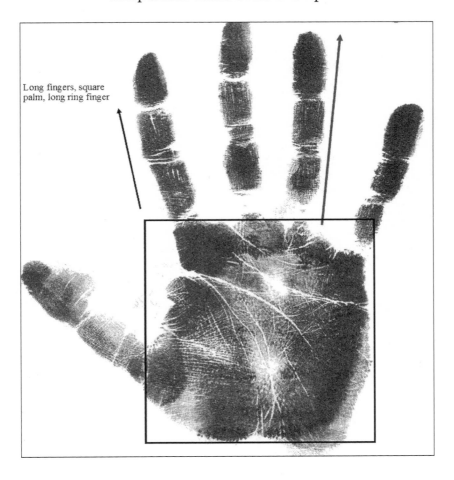

Long fingers, square
palm, long ring finger

Temperance Hand Print Example 2

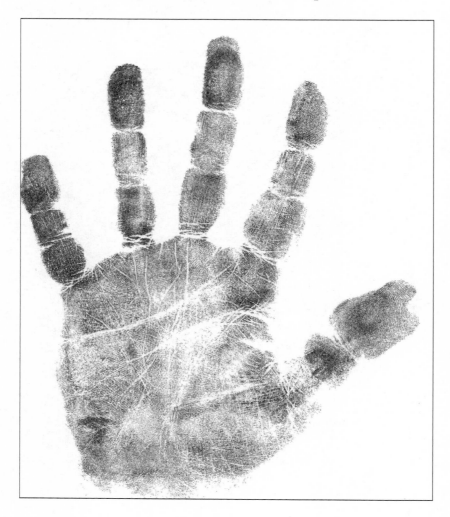

Examples and Exercises

Mudra

To connect to the Temperance archetype in a mudra, place your open palms facing each other with the tips of the little and ring fingers touching each other.

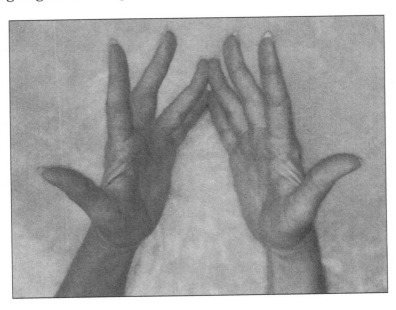

Questions for Growth and Coaches Tips

1. What is too extreme in my life? If you are on the edge in some area of your life, this usually means that another area is suffering or feeling dissatisfied. For example, if you drink too much, it's likely that your relationships are suffering. Examine the extremes to recognize parts of your life that need to heal.

2. What needs adjusting in my life? Use this question to determine areas where you are not fully satisfied. If an adjustment is about another person, look at how you can

change your own attitude rather than trying to change him or her.

3. How can I bring in more of what's really working for me? Look at ways you can invite more of what you want. It helps to write down goals and be specific about the end result. Create a vision board with pictures to represent what you want.

4. What is most balanced in me? This question helps you realize your natural abilities and where you are already strong. Celebrate that. For example, people have told me that I'm able to stay focused even with lots of activity around me. I consider that an asset.

5. How can I bring balance to others? Looking back to your own strengths in question 4, how can you share them with others? For example, maybe you're calm in emergencies. This could be something you teach to others, or offer to those around you in stressful or emergency situations.

Truth Statements for Temperance

1. I adjust my life to stay in balance.
2. I am stabilizing my life now.
3. I easily release extreme tendencies.
4. I let go of rigid thinking and behaviors.
5. I am able to choose action or inaction appropriately.

Chakra Association

Sacral, Heart

Identifying Imbalances

Too much Temperance becomes an inability to decide, not having an opinion or not taking a stance when one is needed.

Too little Temperance results in rigid behavior and thinking without compromise or diplomacy.

Temperance at Home

At home, Temperance is focused on comfort rather than quality or cleanliness. He may not always make his bed, but it feels good at the end of the day and has the right number of blankets on it.

Temperance at Work

It is always easy to get along with Temperance at work. He's the one who listens well and doesn't start an argument. He may not always agree with you, but he handles disputes in a kind and understanding manner. He sometimes wonders why other people get so upset over things. His feathers don't get ruffled easily and he adapts well in any environment.

Temperance in Relationships

In relationships, Temperance does well with a partner who expresses her needs and wants to him. He may not always have a preference for something, so it's better for him to have a partner with stronger opinions who likes to make the plans.

Best Compatibility

Lovers, Hierophant, Wheel of Fortune, Star

Good Compatibility

Fool, Empress, Strength, Justice

Challenging Compatibility

Emperor, Moon, Judgement, Sun

Opposite Archetype

Emperor

Famous Temperance Archetypes

Steven Spielberg, Matt Damon, Orlando Bloom, Elijah Wood, Jack Canfield, Bill Gates, Dolly Parton, Muhammad Ali, Kate Hudson, Kate Middleton

Chapter 15

15–Devil

"Every problem has in it the seeds of its own solution. If you don't have any problems, you don't get any seeds." — Norman Vincent Peale

HAVE YOU EVER HEARD OF THE BOILED FROG story? If a live frog is placed in a pot of boiling water it will immediately jump out. However, if this same frog is placed in cool or lukewarm water and the water is heated slowly to a boil, the frog will remain in the pot and die. The connection of this story to human nature is that we often get caught up in our lives, numb ourselves out and lose a steady awareness to our true selves. Our troubles and fears can be boiling over, but we're not awake to them. They've been building up over time, and we've become so accustomed to that level of existence we don't even remember what we really want anymore. This is our connection to the Devil.

My connection to the Devil occurred shortly before my tenth birthday. There was a video game I wanted and it was all I could think about. The game was made by Atari called "Pitfall." Do any of you remember that game? My parents, being caring and invested in getting me what I wanted for my birthday, surprised me with it. I can still remember how happy and excited I was. I played it over and over for hours. Luckily, my birthday is shortly before Christmas, so I had the entire Christmas vacation to play this game. It was bliss for me in that moment, but ultimately, not productive or moving me in any way toward my true purpose. I was lucky to escape the constant lure of that video game. I'm now able to make new choices for myself that include having fun without becoming addicted.

I had another encounter with the Devil on my thirtieth birthday. I was skiing at Wolf Creek, Colorado, and was talked into hiking a knife-edge ridge to ski some extreme terrain. While I am an expert skier, I do get nervous on ridges, especially when there are drop-offs on both sides, where one could happen to fall to her death. This particular day was cold, cloudy and slightly windy. The boot-pack trail was quite firm and somewhat icy. It was necessary to take my skis off and carry them on my shoulder in order to go up this ridge. Hiking in ski boots does not provide much in the way of traction and I found myself slipping in the icy steps. I could have stopped and turned back, or I could have left the ridge completely alone and just skied elsewhere. Instead, I chose to face my fear, climb the ridge, and ski a beautiful run on the other side. It is by getting out of your comfort zone that you discover your true power.

Physical Attributes

Pictorially, the Devil card resembles the Lovers card, but with a much scarier scene. Here we see the nude man and woman in bondage with a frightening monster behind them, and remarkably an exact image of this archetype's hand. Of course this monster isn't real! To connect with this archetype in the physical world, eat, drink and be merry. Focus on outward beauty and keeping up appearances.

Emotional Attributes

Emotionally, the Devil is about dealing with fear, facing fears and overcoming fears, whether real or imagined. When you let go of your fear and finally recognize the bondage it has over you, a new sense of freedom and empowerment emerges inside of you.

Mental Attributes

Mentally, the Devil archetype is sharp and witty, often using humor to mask pain or fear inside.

Spiritual Attributes

Spiritually, the Devil is more about the material world than the spiritual world. This card represents time before many organized religions. It is associated with Pan, the nature god who took the form of a man-goat.

Key Words for the Devil

Facing fear, cleverness, fun, exuberance, beauty, superficiality, merriment, excess

Palmistry Identification

Air + Mercury

In the hands, the Devil archetype is represented by the following combination: long fingers, square palm, Air, and long little finger, Mercury. Here are hand print examples of the Devil archetype:

Devil Hand Print Example 1

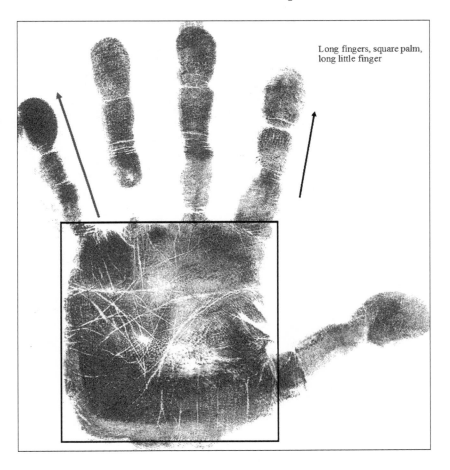

Long fingers, square palm, long little finger

Devil Hand Print Example 2

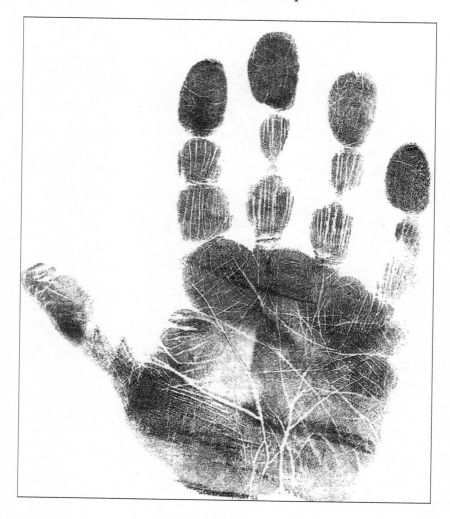

Examples and Exercises

Mudra

To connect to the Devil archetype in a mudra, place your little fingers straight and touching each other at the tips. Curl the other fingers inward at the lower knuckles and touch the thumbs together at the tips.

Questions for Growth and Coaches Tips

1. What fears do I need to release? Just because you don't encounter a certain fear every day, such as a fear of heights, does not mean that it wouldn't be better to release it. Take a deep look at all your fears, including when and how they emerged.
2. In what ways do I overindulge? Analyzing your excesses can help you to recognize what needs to change. Through practice, you can make anything unfamiliar.

For example, if you are addicted to sugar in your coffee in the morning, try cutting it out completely for two weeks. During that time, tell yourself you are choosing to like black coffee instead.

3. In what ways do I restrict myself in indulging? This can be equally problematic if you never allow yourself to have something you enjoy. The key is finding and living in balance. Maybe you love chocolate, but never allow yourself to have it. Life is not meant to be a complete restriction. Go ahead and have some once in a while. Just be sure to enjoy and appreciate it when you do, rather than beat yourself up afterward.

4. How can I use humor in a positive way today? Make it a habit to lighten up. Many people take life and themselves too seriously. Listen to a comedy channel, read or tell a joke, watch a funny video. Laughter helps raise your vibration level, so it's easier to release fear or anxiety.

5. What do I find beautiful and why? Take some time to identify your definition of beauty. As you become more mindful of it, you'll gradually return to a state of gratitude. Do you have this beauty around you? If not, how can you bring it in? For example, if you find flowers beautiful, do you ever buy flowers and place them in your office or kitchen? What about with your own body? What part do you find the most beautiful? Take time to appreciate it.

Truth Statements for the Devil

1. I am willing and able to release my fears.
2. I am connected with my inner and outer beauty.
3. I balance my indulgences in a way that works for me.
4. I create and appreciate beauty around me.
5. I allow myself to have fun and be playful every day.

Chakra Association

Root, Throat

Identifying Imbalances

Too much Devil results in debauchery and addictive behavior. This can be from a refusal to conquer fears. Too little Devil results in denial, especially of physical pleasures. There can be a harsh judgment associated here, often including guilt and self-loathing.

The Devil at Home

At home, the Devil creates a space filled with all the material indulgences that interest him. If he's into technology, for example, he will have all the latest gadgets at his fingertips. If he's into cooking, he will have a huge kitchen filled with all the latest appliances.

The Devil at Work

At work, the Devil moves so fast, it's hard for others to keep up with him. He's extremely clever and witty, but perhaps a bit sharp for most people. He's edgy and intense, unless he's worked on toning this part of himself down. He is highly skilled at his craft, whatever he chooses to do, but he may be a bit clueless in other areas of his life.

The Devil in Relationships

In relationships, it's hard for the Devil to get too serious for too long unless he's worked deeply on himself. Underneath, he has some deep seeded insecurities and he needs to work through these with a loving and understanding partner. If he's evolved in this challenging archetype, he will find a partner who appreciates his sense of humor and can keep up with his astute observations without taking offense. He can be incredibly playful and fun to be around when he's feeling good about himself and his life.

Best Compatibility

Fool, Chariot, Death

Good Compatibility

Magician, Hanged Man, Tower

Challenging Compatibility

High Priestess, Empress, Emperor, Hierophant, Hermit, Justice, Sun

Opposite Archetype

Empress

Famous Devil Archetypes

Robin Williams, Hugh Jackman, Tom Cruise, Mahatma Gandhi, Richard Nixon, Natalie Wood

Chapter 16

16–Tower

"The more we can purge ourselves of the diseases we create, the more we can become magnificent people." — Judith Light

BACK IN THE 1990'S, MY FORMER HUSBAND AND I were trying to start our own restaurant. Both of us had extensive backgrounds in food service, and at the time I was working at Starbucks in the Salt Lake City airport. I had already obtained my business management degree from the University of Utah, so I figured it wouldn't be too hard to get this new venture going.

It took us two years of preparation, a roller coaster ride through unraveling partnerships, and a bank loan that fell through in the eleventh hour. This was my encounter with the Tower. Needless to say, I was completely devastated and beginning to think that our dream wasn't going to happen. But somehow my heart was still telling me it was going to be work out.

My intuition was right. We soon heard back from one of our contacts in southern Utah where we were planning on opening our store. A new opportunity emerged and we took it. Even though things didn't turn out the way we'd initially envisioned them, our plans materialized and we opened our cafe in the summer of 1999. This struggle through adversity and doubt helped me to realize that if you stay confident and positive in your heart, miracles can happen in your life. Looking back on it now, I'm grateful for the way things evolved in ways that were appropriate for us at the time. The purging and purification of the birth of our business went exactly as it needed to.

Physical Attributes

The Tower card is another frightening looking card depicting a burning tower with two people plunging to their deaths. Physically, to connect to this card, it's about eliminating what no longer works for you. For example, get rid of old clothes, old papers or old technology to make room for something better.

Emotional Attributes

Emotionally, the Tower is about purging unwanted emotions such as anger, frustration, fear or worries. These emotions only hold you back from being your authentic self. Think of this process as a purification, burning out of you what needs to release.

Mental Attributes

Mentally, the Tower is about awakening through unexpected circumstances. Your house burning down may seem like a horrible incident, but maybe it leads you to move to a much more beautiful and spacious home in a different part of the country where you find your soul mate. Looking back, you say that the incident was the best thing that ever happened to you. Searching for silver linings creates more silver in your life.

Spiritual Attributes

Spiritually, the Tower is ultimately teaching you to be purified and look at the disasters of your life as opportunities for greater growth and enlightenment. Understanding that the earth plane is temporary, but your soul is eternal can help you gain perspective.

Key Words for the Tower

Truth, illumination, shock, purging, rebuilding, restructuring, purifying

Palmistry Identification

Air + Fire

In the hands, the Tower archetype is represented by two elements which can appear in the hands in two ways: long fingers, square palm, Air, with deep, numerous lines or short fingers, rectangular palm, Fire, with numerous, fine and clear lines. Here are hand print examples of the Tower archetype, both with Fire hands and Air lines:

The Tower Hand Print Example 1

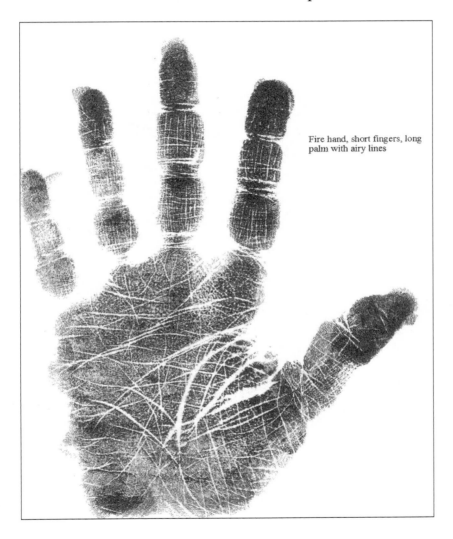

Fire hand, short fingers, long palm with airy lines

The Tower Hand Print Example 2

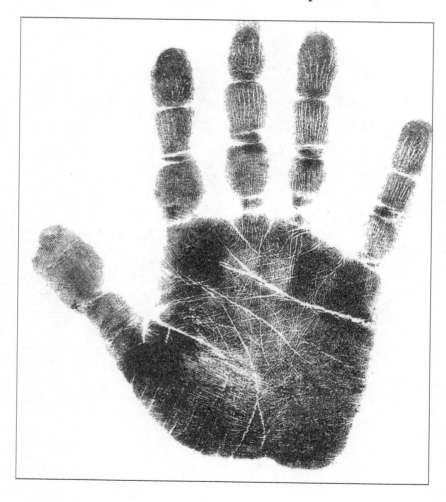

Examples & Exercises

Mudra

To connect to the Tower in a mudra, place your index and little fingers together, pointing straight, with all the other fingers curled in.

Questions for Growth and Coaches Tips

1. What keeps nagging me to change? One way to answer this question is to evaluate the relationships in your life. Do you keep hearing the same advice from more than one person? Instead of brushing it off, could it be possible that they are right?
2. What negative, repetitive thoughts am I having? This is so automatic, so unconscious, that you need to pay close attention. Sometimes it's easier to look at situations that create stress for you. For example, is there someone at work you argue constantly with, or do you dread rush hour traffic every day? What are your thoughts around these situations?

3. What negative emotions keep coming up for me? Are
    you consistently sad, angry, frustrated or anxious? Do
    you have enough energy in the day to be productive and
    happy? Once you identify your temperament, ask your-
    self if there is one thing you can do to shift it? Then take
    that action.
4. What illness (es) do I have? What are they trying to tell
    me? Illnesses are always trying to tell you something.
    The body naturally wants to be healthy. An illness is
    simply showing you that something needs to change.
    Pay attention to the location of the illness. For example,
    a foot problem may indicate a lack of grounding. A head
    injury could relate to a desire to forget a painful expe-
    rience from your past. A cut may be telling you that an
    emotion you've been holding in wants to bleed out.
5. What can I purify in my mind, body or spirit right now?
    Once you identify some of these negative influences, here
    is an easy activity for you. Go out into the sunlight and
    envision the rays of light penetrating your cells and pu-
    rifying your toxins, like a sunlight bath. Close your eyes
    and face the sun. Inhale the beautiful rays, let the heat
    burn off and disintegrate anything you want to purge.
    Exhale the toxic energy, returning it to the atmosphere
    to be transmuted. Do this for several minutes until you
    feel clean and pure.

Truth Statements for the Tower

1. Every event in my life leads me to greater understanding
    and authenticity.
2. I grow and learn from all challenges in my life.
3. I allow myself to be purified in my mind, body and spirit.
4. I let go of imbalances in my energy field.
5. My life is getting better and better through all experiences.

Chakra Association

Third Eye, Crown

Identifying Imbalances

Too much Tower results in an inability to restructure or grow from life challenges, usually resulting in a need to repeat a lesson with a similar scenario. Too little Tower is all about hoarding and holding on to things far past their usefulness.

The Tower at Home

The Tower prefers to move around, not keeping anything at home too permanent. He may have a permanent home, but the way it looks changes from year to year or even month to month. He is also quite happy traveling, since a change in scenery results in a change in energy.

The Tower at Work

At work, the Tower may appear as quite a dynamo to others. He has lots of energy and prefers to work on his own terms. He may be quite brilliant in his field of expertise, but gets tripped up periodically in other areas that affect his work. If you ask him, he's happy to share his knowledge and expertise with you.

The Tower in Relationships

In relationships, the Tower benefits from a partner who can calm and ground him. He has a hard time relaxing and just letting himself chill. Always moving and doing something, he prefers a partner with a lot of energy or the ability to be alone and do his own thing.

Best Compatibility

Strength, Hanged Man, Judgement

Good Compatibility

Magician, Lovers, Chariot, Sun, World

Challenging Compatibility

Fool, High Priestess, Empress, Emperor, Hermit, Justice, Moon

Opposite Archetype

Moon

Famous Tower Archetypes

Albert Einstein, Michael Jackson, Morpheus

Chapter 17

17–Star

"Passion is born the moment you catch a glimpse of your potential." — Fred Smith

ONE OF THE BEAUTIFUL THINGS ABOUT HANDS IS
the way they show you what your talents are, whether latent or
fully developed. In my own hands, I discovered that I possess a
marker known as the "healing stigmata." This particular talent
imparts various healing gifts to its owner, and how it manifests
can vary tremendously from person to person. At the time I
learned about this marker, I wasn't yet sure how it might actually be used. This is often the case when we first discover a
definitive marker.

I came in touch with the Star in late 2009. I was reading a
book on energy healing, and as I was reading it I felt something
getting sucked into my hands – first my left hand and then my
right. My hands felt hot and tingly, like the pins and needles you
feel when part of your body "falls asleep," cutting off its circula-
tion. It was such a strange experience. All I could do was stare
at my hands and wonder what had just happened.

After a few minutes of staring at my hands, I decided to
test out the information I was reading on various people in my
life. One person had endured back pain for most of his life, so I
asked him if I could experiment with this "energy." He agreed,
and within two minutes the pain in his back dissipated. Another
was struggling with a knee injury, and again, the pain decreased
within just a few minutes of testing my process. These experiences eventually led me to helping others in the same way. I
chose to follow the pathway and open up to being a catalyst for
others to heal.

Physical Attributes

The Star card depicts a nude woman, indicating honesty
and purity. She is transferring water from a pond to the earth.
There are seven small stars above her and one large star. There
is a bird in a tree in the background. To physically connect with
this archetype, you need to be in touch with your luminosity.

Dress and present yourself in a way that makes you feel honest and pure.

Emotional Attributes

Emotionally, the Star uses her beauty to help others see theirs. She is transferring information from the subconscious (the water) to the conscious (the earth.) Become emotionally attuned to your own talents. What do you enjoy doing naturally?

Mental Attributes

Mentally, the Star is about identifying and developing talents and dreams. When you wish upon a star, you are mentally acknowledging a desire. Desires of a higher calling are meant to be developed; that's why they take root inside you to begin with.

Spiritual Attributes

Spiritually, the Star is a dreamer. She happily dips into the subconscious possibilities and brings them to the surface to be exposed and developed. The bird behind her is showing the freedom of infinite possibilities. It is asking her, "how would you like to fly?"

Key Words for the Star

Desires, talents, luminous, fame, dreams, possibility

Palmistry Identification

Air + Water

In the hands, the Star archetype is represented by two elements which can appear in the hands in two ways: long fingers, square palm, Air, with fine, delicate, numerous lines, or long fingers, rectangular palm, Water, with numerous, fine and clear lines. Here are hand print examples of the Star archetype, both of which depict an Air hand with Water lines:

The Star Hand Print Example 1

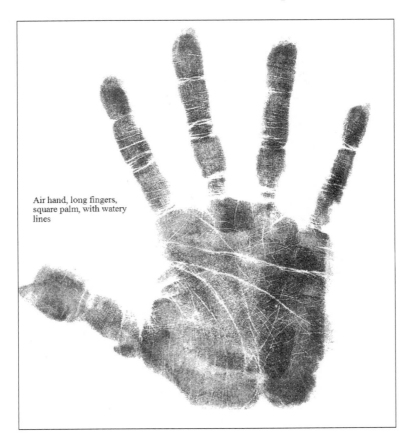

Air hand, long fingers, square palm, with watery lines

The Star Hand Print Example 2

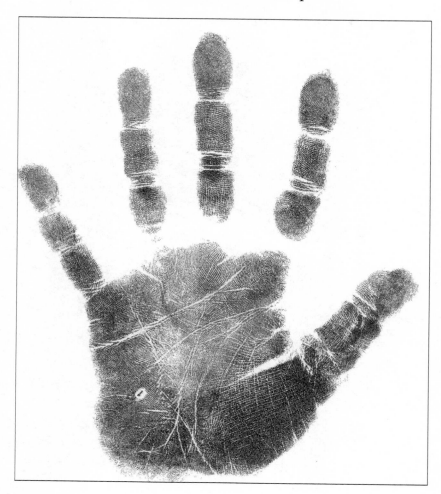

Examples and Exercises

Mudra

To connect to the Star archetype in a mudra, place your palms open with the thumbs out and the upper ring fingers touching each other. Place the middle and index fingers straight and locked together next to the ring fingers. Lower the little fingers to the base of the palm, farthest away from the thumb, touching the palm.

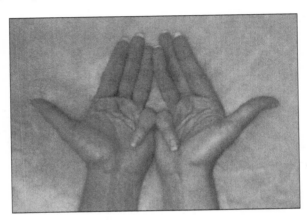

Questions for Growth and Coaches Tips

1. What do I dream about doing or being? Take some time to fantasize and don't worry about whether it's realistic or not.
2. What talents do I have that still wish to be developed further? Look at your hobbies, or areas of your life that are only partially developed. Hobbies often turn into careers because they start as a passion or interest.
3. How can I help other people see and use their talents? Take some time with the people closest to you and acknowledge them for what they are naturally good at. Encouragement goes a long way in building confidence

and allowing another person to step out of his or her own comfort zone. We can all use encouragement.

4. What talents am I currently using? Evaluate what you're doing already. Does it bring you joy? If it doesn't, then it may be time for a change.

5. How am I beautiful? Recognizing your own beauty is the first step to realizing your dreams. You aren't doing anyone any favors by staying small and ugly. If you don't see anything beautiful about yourself, ask your mother or your best friend what they see.

Truth Statements for the Star

1. I am in touch with my dreams.
2. I take time to daydream and fantasize.
3. I am developing my talents and gifts.
4. I assist others in seeing and using their talents.
5. I envision the best possibilities for myself and others.

Chakra Association

Sacral, Solar Plexus

Identifying Imbalances

Too much Star results in knowing your talents, but not developing them. Too little Star is about not seeing or knowing your talents at all.

The Star at Home

At home, the Star exudes her beauty without even realizing all that it truly is. She is gracious, thoughtful about her emotions, quiet yet present. She takes her time with things, sometimes not getting to every chore. She enjoys reading and possibly writing. Journaling and meditating benefit her and keep her balanced.

The Star at Work

At work, the Star knows what she's good at, and takes her time in fully developing herself to be the best in her craft. She doesn't expect to get there immediately. Her work is a long term investment. It's much better for her not to have a strict schedule; the flexibility allows her to change her plans according to the mood of the day, although she is fully capable of meeting a deadline. She works just fine on her own, but really shines when she's able to motivate her coworkers. That's easy for her.

The Star in Relationships

The Star makes a gentle and thoughtful lover. She can be very romantic and brings a calm security to her partner. She encourages the sharing of needs and desires, and easily creates this awareness in her relationship. Sometimes, she can become sad or overly serious as dreams take time to manifest. When this occurs, she needs a partner who can bring her joy and help her see her own beauty.

Best Compatibility

High Priestess, Strength, Temperance

Good Compatibility

Fool, Empress, Hierophant, Hermit, Death, Sun

Challenging Compatibility

Lovers, Wheel of Fortune, Justice, Moon, World

Opposite Archetype

World

Famous Star Archetypes

Robin Williams, Jack Canfield, Matt Damon, Hugh Jackman, David Beckham, Steve Jobs, Ellen Degeneres

Chapter 18

18–Moon

"As soon as you trust yourself you will know how to live." – Johann Wolfgang von Goethe

I'VE ALWAYS HAD A DEEP AFFILIATION WITH THE Moon. My name, Cynthia, has derivatives – Cindy, Cintha, Thea, Tia, Lucinda and Lucille – all relating to the moon, after the Greek goddess Artemis, twin sister of Apollo. For most of my life, I was a night owl. I found myself doing much of my writing and creative work late at night when it was quiet and no one would disturb me. I loved looking up at the moon and the stars. It would help me expand into the realm of infinite possibilities. In fact, it saddens me that many people who now live in cities can't see the beautiful night sky and all its dazzling mysteries due to our global light pollution epidemic. There is something very special about gazing into the vastness of space, and many people have lost this connection.

There is a ritual I perform in rhythm with the Moon. To me, the new moon represents a time of new beginnings. I like to write out ten affirmations within three days of the new moon that I feel are important to focus on for the entire month. I read them every day, and when the moon is full I go back and evaluate how many of my aspirations have come to pass or progressed in any way. I bring in gratitude regarding my progress. This connection to the Moon archetype helps me to be more reflective and mindful. There's something powerful in setting intentions. It shows the universe that we're serious about what we want and willing to take a few extra steps to align us with our goals.

Physical Attributes

The Moon card depicts a large, luminous moon in between two towers. There is a dog and a coyote howling up at it, appearing agitated. A lobster is coming out of a body of water. Physically, the moon represents the feminine principle and the nature of cycles. To connect to the Moon, dress in a way that is appropriate for the occasion. Sometimes you may feel like bold, bright colors. Other times, you may prefer to wear black. How you dress and present yourself affects not only how you are seen by others, but your mood and mental state as well.

Emotional Attributes

Emotionally, the Moon is still and reflective, as shown by the two towers in the card. There are emotional aspects that are kept hidden.

Mental Attributes

Mentally, the Moon is showing you the influences of your subconscious, as depicted by the animals. Whether you like it or not, your subconscious mind is driving about ninety-five percent of your actions, while your conscious mind is driving the other five percent. When you consider your life from this perspective, you can clearly see the importance of the subconscious mind.

Spiritual Attributes

Spiritually, the Moon is about cycles and phases. During the new moon, you are starting a new phase, new beginnings. The full moon is about the harvest. Between the new moon and the full moon, you have your consciousness growing and expanding as you develop an idea to its manifestation. As the moon wanes, the cycle retreats, and you go within to regroup until the next cycle begins.

Key Words for the Moon

Hidden, subconscious, cyclical, phases, symbolism

Palmistry Identification

Earth + Water

In the hands, the Moon archetype is represented by two elements which can appear in the hands in two ways: short fingers, square palm, Earth, with fine, delicate, numerous lines; or long fingers, rectangular palm, Water, with just a few deep lines. Here are hand print examples of the Moon archetype, shown as Earth hands with Water lines:

The Moon Hand Print Example 1

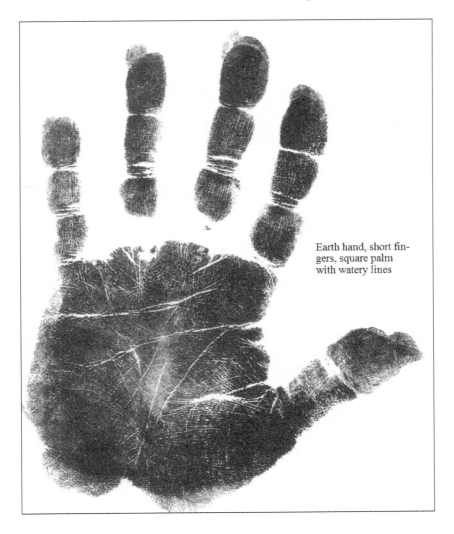

Earth hand, short fingers, square palm with watery lines

The Moon Hand Print Example 2

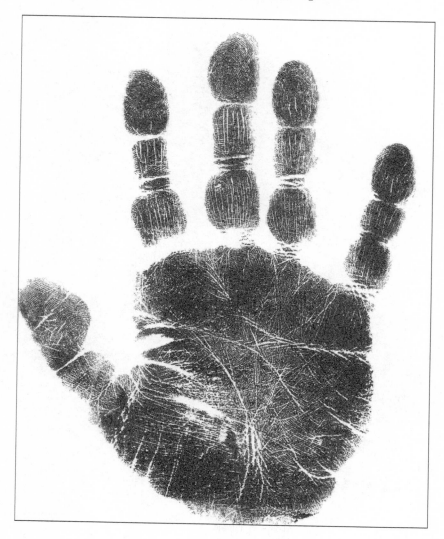

Examples and Exercises

Mudra

To connect to the Moon archetype in a mudra, place your palms up with all four fingers closed over each palm surface. Place the thumbs straight out and touch the percussion of each hand together.

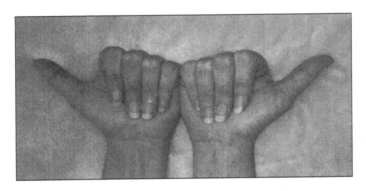

Questions for Growth and Coaches Tips

1. How can I use cycles to live more authentically? Look at cycles through the lens of nature. Besides the cycles of the moon, look at the four seasons, planetary alignments, animal behavior, tides and weather.
2. What cycle am I currently in now? Look at your biological age and what's going on in your life right now. Look at where you live and what seems to be happening around you. For example, do you have construction on the street where you live? This could be an indication of expecting delays in other areas of your life too. Find parallels.
3. What cycle would I like to change in my life? Sticking with the age example, you may not be able to change your biological age, but you can change your attitude about what it means to be that age. In fact, you actually

have two ages: your biological age and your designated age. In other words, how old or young do you feel inside? When you change your belief around something, you can change the cycle.

4. How can I work with the moon's cycles to correspond with my life? Get a calendar that lists the cycles of the moon. Mark them in your own planner. Set up your own rituals over the course of these cycles. Notice how you feel during different moon phases. Is there a time when you're more social? When you tend to withdraw? Is your sleep affected?

5. What is hidden from me that needs to come to light? This is answered best in meditation and quiet reflection. Then look for signs in your environment.

Truth Statements for the Moon

1. I work with the natural cycles of my body.
2. I work with the natural cycles of nature.
3. I trust in the cycles of my life to be just right for me.
4. I balance my life in cycles.
5. I connect to the power of the moon's energy each night.

Chakra Association

Sacral

Identifying Imbalances

Too much Moon results in "lunacy," not seeing things as they are. This can produce all sorts of issues such as over-reacting or creating problems that don't really exist. It can create paranoia, withdrawal or isolation. Too little Moon results in living out of balance with the cycles of nature and what is appropriate for you. If you are trying to force something to happen, even if the timing is obviously poor, this is an example of deficient Moon energy.

The Moon at Home

At home, the Moon displays appropriate décor for the occasion or time of year. She changes things up so you always know what season it is and where she is at in her own stage of life.

The Moon at Work

At work, the Moon is nurturing and receptive. She absorbs and gathers information to be used at a later time. She enjoys working with others in a cooperative fashion, but is also capable of spending time alone in her office to organize and reflect.

The Moon in Relationships

In relationships, it is easy to lean on the Moon person. She is understanding of her partner's needs and innately knows how to calm his stress. She loves romantic evenings inside, with plenty of massage oil and wine or chocolate. She is physically sensual and enjoys using her sense of touch in deep and playful ways. She is also very aware of her own needs and cycles. When she needs time to herself, she needs an understanding partner who is not threatened or judgmental.

Best Compatibility

High Priestess, Wheel of Fortune, Hanged Man, Judgement

Good Compatibility

Empress, Hermit, Justice, Death

Challenging Compatibility

Magician, Hierophant, Lovers, Chariot, Tower, Star, World

Opposite Archetype

Tower

Famous Moon Archetypes

Prince William, Dennis Hopper, Justin Bieber, George H.W. Bush, Donald Trump, Dr. Jekyll

Chapter 19

19–Sun

"There are two ways of spreading light: to be the candle
or the mirror that reflects it." — Edith Wharton

MY CONNECTION TO THE SUN OCCURRED ON A dark wintery day in February. I had been going through a traumatic time in my life and was feeling depressed. I was in a large metaphysical gift shop in Salt Lake City waiting for a client to do my next reading. This particular store has a huge open area just past the front door, a great place to wait for and meet people. As I was waiting, an elderly Native American woman whom I had never seen before walked up to me and said she had a message to deliver to me. She placed one of her hands on my forehead and the other on my chest. She closed her eyes and breathed deeply. After a few moments, she opened her eyes and removed her hands. Then she said, "You are about to go on a huge adventure. You have a good heart. Everything's going to be ok." Then she walked away.

This encounter left me speechless. Who was this mysterious woman who could see into my soul and deliver a comforting message during a dark period of my life? Maybe she was an angel. I will never know for sure, but I do know I was touched that day by the Sun.

Physical Attributes

The Sun card shows a young boy, nude, on a white horse waving a banner of victory. Above him is a brilliantly shining sun with sunflowers blooming behind him. To physically align yourself to this archetype, wear what makes you feel radiant so that others take notice. Wear bright, "sunny" colors or flashy jewelry. Pay special attention to your hair, makeup, shoes and accessories.

Emotional Attributes

Emotionally, the Sun is optimistic, as indicated by the nude boy. He knows that he's victorious and feels fantastic, strong and invincible. Go back to a time in your life when you were victorious. Did you ever win a competition? Reflect on how you felt during that time.

Mental Attributes

Mentally, the Sun is about creating light. As you shine your light outward, you disperse shadows around you so that others may see their light too. Be optimistic.

Spiritual Attributes

Spiritually, the Sun knows the light. He knows he is light; he creates light and he spreads light. He represents the positive attributes of enlightenment, spreading love, joy and understanding.

Key Words for the Sun

Radiant, glowing, optimistic, shining, hot, creative

Palmistry Identification

Earth + Apollo

In the hands, the Sun archetype is represented by the following combination: short fingers, square palm, Earth, and long ring finger, Apollo. Here are hand print examples of the Sun archetype:

The Sun Hand Print Example 1

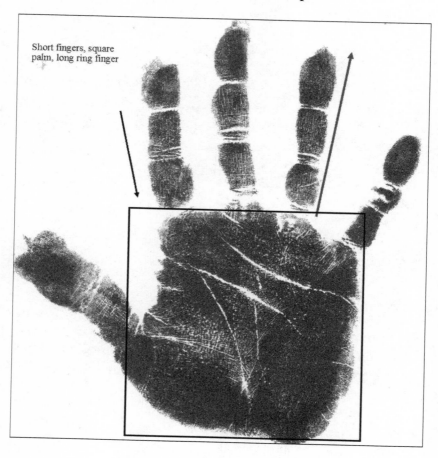

Short fingers, square palm, long ring finger

The Sun Hand Print Example 2

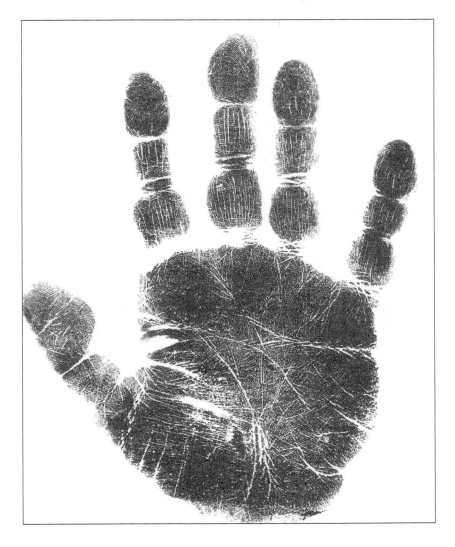

Examples and Exercises

Mudra

To connect to the Sun archetype in a mudra, place open palms facing each other with the tips of the ring fingers touching each other.

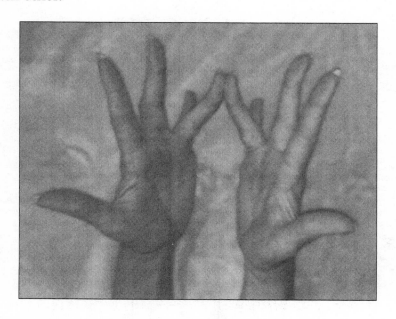

Questions for Growth and Coaches Tips

1. What can I be more optimistic about? Take a close look at areas of your life such as your body, your relationships, your finances, your friends. Do you spend a lot of time watching the news and worrying about the state of global affairs? It's one thing to be informed, but what you focus on expands. Focus on the light, not the darkness.
2. What can I do to improve my physical appearance? Examine your body closely and evaluate all your parts neutrally. Maybe your teeth are crooked or you have a

wart or a mole on your body. Maybe you're just over-weight. Decide how you'd like your body to look instead. What's one step you can take to create that change?

3. How can I create light for someone else today? Little acts of kindness go a long way. Say please and thank you to those you interact with. Write thank you on a bill you're paying. Pay someone's expired parking meter. Take out your neighbor's trash. Smile everywhere you go.

4. What truth about myself do I know and not acknowl-edge? Take time to appreciate and love yourself. What are doing right now that's great and valuable? Going back to your body, what parts do you love?

5. How can I create more light for myself? Physically, you can brighten a room with flowers, colors, textures and lamps. Emotionally focus on joy and love. Mentally focus on the outcomes you want to see happen. Spiritually, take time to appreciate your own inner light.

Truth Statements for the Sun

1. I know that I am fully supported by the universe at all times.
2. I acknowledge my own brilliance.
3. I am willing and able to show my greatness to others.
4. I spread radiance everywhere I go.
5. I am a magnet to the light.

Chakra Association

Solar Plexus, Heart, Throat

Identifying Imbalances

Too much Sun results in burning others, overwhelming them in some way that blocks the emergence of their full po-tential. This can occur in various ways, by being judgmental or insulting, superior or angry. Too little Sun results in pessimism and depression. You may not be able to know your own worth or develop your potential.

The Sun at Home

At home, the Sun enjoys lots of windows to let in natural light. He also enjoys spending as much time outdoors as indoors. He has a tremendous amount of energy available to him, so he also needs a physical outlet that is aerobic in nature, like running, skiing, biking, or hiking. If he doesn't use this energy, he may get depressed or take it out on others in a negative way.

The Sun at Work

At work, the Sun is very creative and loves to express this creativity to others who can appreciate it. He works quickly and efficiently, making it hard for others without this archetype to keep up sometimes. He gets bored easily, so he needs work that continues to challenge and stimulate him. He has high standards for the quality of his work and expects perfection. He may feel underappreciated for his work.

The Sun in Relationships

The Sun makes an exciting and energetic partner. He appreciates music, concerts and creative meals. He is open to trying new things, but can also be loyal to what works for him. He sees and acknowledges the qualities he values in his partner. This builds her security and affection. He helps her to shine her own light and be herself. His optimism is contagious, making him popular with his inner circle of friends as well.

Best Compatibility

Magician, Lovers, World

Good Compatibility

Empress, Hierophant, Chariot, Hermit, Wheel of Fortune, Justice

Challenging Compatibility

Fool, Strength, Temperance, Devil

Opposite Archetype

Strength

Famous Sun Archetypes

Ronald Reagan, Magic Johnson, Nelson Mandela, Anthony Robbins, Peyton Manning, Dennis Hopper

Chapter 20

20–Judgement

"How people treat you is their karma; how
you react is yours." — Wayne Dyer

I'VE HAD MANY JOBS IN MY LIFETIME. FOR A PE-riod of about three years, I worked for the United States Postal Service as a "remote encoder." The Postal Service receives handwritten mail each day that can't be read by the automatic bar code sorters. As a remote encoder, I saw a photo of a piece of mail on a computer screen. I would enter in appropriate information so the bar code could be printed at the bottom of the envelope and the mail could continue to its destination.

Although not a glamorous job, it was at the time good paying work that I was skilled at. My keying ability was fast and accurate, but after a couple of years, the job started to bore me. I was not challenged in the least, nor was I ever planning on moving up within the facility. This was just a part time job while I was in college, and as my attitude toward it changed I began connecting to Judgement. The longer I stayed, the more I knew that something else was waiting for me. During the last six months on the job, I continually had an uneasy, unsettled feeling. There was a gnawing in my stomach, an anxiety that begged for relief. Even though nothing had changed with the job – it was still as predictable as ever – there was a change happening inside me. When I finally claimed my personal power, and decided the time was right, I quit and started a new, more interesting job, even though it paid less money.

Physical Attributes

The Judgement card depicts an angel blowing a horn to a crowd of nude gray souls, both younger and slightly older, holding their arms up to him, as if they are recently resurrected. Of course, this is not about actual death, because death is not typically recognized either in tarot or palmistry. To align physically to this archetype, claim power over your own body and see the possibility of total health. Recognize that illness is just a way to get your attention so that you may transform.

Emotional Attributes

Emotionally, Judgement is reflective and honest. He shows you what's real for you in this moment. He is a truth mirror. He asks you to release and transform for your highest expression to emerge. When you finally recognize your own limitations for what they are – *limitations,* then you may shift into a new emotional state and be free. Some common limitations include *I'm not good enough; Who am I to do that?; It's not perfect, so why even try; I'll never have that; It's impossible; I don't deserve that; I'm such a loser.* Recognize these as the shackles that hold you back and let them go.

Mental Attributes

Mentally, Judgement knows where he's been and where he's going. He is determined to purify his limiting thoughts so he may be transformed. *I am good enough; I can do this; It's brilliant; I am having that; It's possible; I deserve that; I'm a winner.*

Spiritual Attributes

Spiritually, Judgement is accepting of karma. He recognizes that his thoughts create his reality. He strives for enlightenment and purification as his life progresses, knowing that his actions have consequences for his own joy and satisfaction. He knows that by hurting others, he is only hurting himself.

Key Words for Judgement

Resurrection, transformation, personal power, release, blossoming

Palmistry Identification

Earth + Air

In the hands, the Judgement archetype is represented by two elements which can appear in the hands in two ways: short fingers, square palm, Earth, with fine, clear, numerous lines or long fingers, square palm, Air, with just a few deep lines. Here are hand print examples of the Judgement archetype, both depicting the Earth hand shape and Air lines:

Judgement Hand Print Example 1

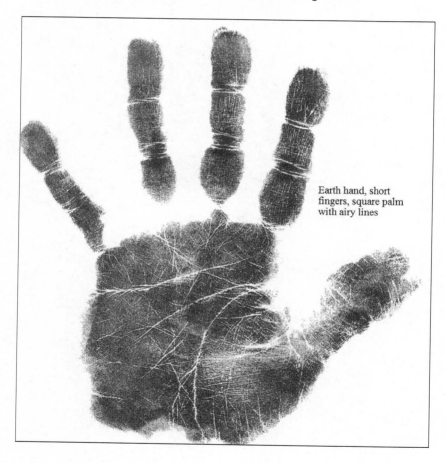

Earth hand, short fingers, square palm with airy lines

Judgement Hand Print Example 2

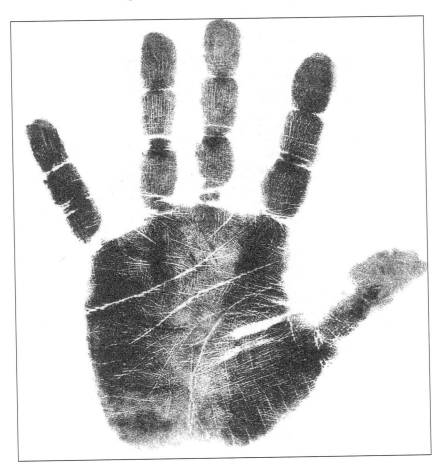

Examples and Exercises

Mudra

Place the fingertips together on each hand of the index, middle and ring fingers. Bend the little fingers and touch them to the thumbs with all four of these fingers touching.

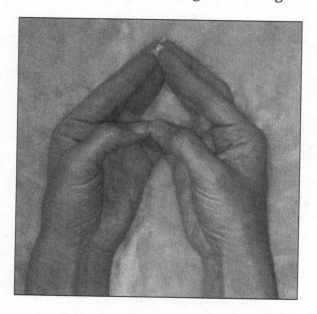

Questions for Growth and Coaches Tips

1. How can I love and accept where I'm at right now in my life? Be in a state of gratitude for all that you have accomplished up to this point. If you could have done anything differently, you would have. This question is about letting go of regrets.

2. In what ways do I see myself as less than a magnificent person? How do you currently beat yourself up? Recognize your own imposed limitations. For example, many people are critical of their weight. Look below

the physical and know the soul that resides in the body. Bring love and compassion to yourself at all times.

3. What have I not done yet? Looking at your life as a progression, your soul wishes to expand. What do you long to do?

4. Who and what do I judge? Your own judgements show you areas that would like to heal within yourself. For instance, if you are critical and judgmental of other people's looks, this simply means that you feel insecure and unloving within yourself, and you're projecting this outward toward others. Have you noticed that people who really love themselves don't have a need to judge others?

5. What judgements can I release now? Change your limitations to be reframed in a more empowering way. Focus on the outcomes you seek. For example, let's say you hold a bitter opinion of your sister because she was always mean to you when you were little. If you reframe that bitterness to recognize that both of you held wounded beliefs about yourselves, you can transform the bitterness to love. Recognize your own self-loathing, that was reinforced by her behavior toward you. Recognize her own insecurity that she picked on you to make herself feel more important. Transform the insecurity and self-loathing and all that's left is love, nurturing the ability to be more in alignment with your true self.

Truth Statements for Judgement

1. I love and accept myself exactly as I am.
2. I love and accept others regardless of their actions.
3. I honor and cherish my growth levels.
4. I release judgement of myself and others.
5. I allow the universe to guide me in my next steps.

Chakra Association

Throat, Third Eye

Identifying Imbalances

Too much Judgement results in forcing or rejecting the proper time and space for your own growth and development. It's about holding on to limitations and not being able to recognize them as invitations to transform. Too little Judgement results in ignorance around your journey, not knowing or reflecting on your actions or the consequences of your actions.

Judgement at Home

At home, Judgement is aware of how furnishings affect a space. He is balanced when things are put where they belong and are not too cramped. He enjoys being at home, but also enjoys having company over and entertaining with fine food and beverages.

Judgement at Work

At work, Judgement comes up with practical ideas and knows the best way to implement them. He takes his work seriously and does better with meaningful work. He uses his past mistakes to create a better future for himself and those around him. He recognizes when it's time to move on either within a job or to a new position entirely.

Judgement in Relationships

Judgement understands his partner and is empathetic to what she has gone through before. He is not afraid to point out challenges, but offers them as solutions for making everyone's life better. He may be quick to progress a relationship in some ways but not others. He likes to be the one to lead in the relationship, especially concerning the rate of development. He learns from his own mistakes and expects others to do the same.

Best Compatibility

Chariot, Justice, Tower, Moon

Good Compatibility

Fool, High Priestess, Hierophant, Wheel of Fortune, Death

Challenging Compatibility

Magician, Lovers, Strength, Temperance

Opposite Archetype

None, just like the Hanged Man, Judgement contains opposing elements, this time with earth and air

Famous Judgement Archetypes

Elijah Wood, Oprah Winfrey, Nelson Mandela, Denzel Washington, Yassir Arafat

Chapter 21

21–World

"You were designed for accomplishment,
engineered for success, and endowed with
the seeds of greatness." — Zig Ziglar

THE MORE HANDS I ANALYZE, THE MORE I REAL-
ize that we are all different and unique, yet we are also all the same. We are here doing what we can to get through life and complete our purpose. What do we have in common? We own a pair of hands, at least most of us anyway. But no two hands are alike; each one is a completely unique expression of its owner, showing possibility and potential. Every time I look at some- one's hand, I am connected to the World. Knowing my own archetypes has taught me that I cannot ignore my responsibility to awaken as many people as possible to their authentic selves. What waits for them in their own full potential as spiritual beings having a human experience is expressed through the shape and markings of their beautiful hands. No one else in the world can be you. No one else in the world can fulfill your calling and purpose. I hope that finding and living your life with this knowledge empowers you to seek the greatness within you and share it with the World.

Physical Attributes

The final card of the Major Arcana, the World, brings you to a place of inner and outer beauty. This card depicts a gentle nude dancing woman holding two wands. She is surrounded by a lion, a bird, a cow and a man. To connect with this archetype physically, bring awareness to your own beauty, both inner and outer, and to the expansive beauty of the planet. Connect to your pets, nature, plants and other people of all races and back- grounds. Take time to bless the earth for supporting you in this physical realm.

Emotional Attributes

Emotionally, the World is about the concept of oneness. We are all here together on this journey and to support each other and love each other as members of this planet. Feel your own interconnectedness.

Mental Attributes

Mentally, the World is focused on humanitarian responsibilities. How you think and act affects everyone and everything around you. Ask yourself how you can be a better person as a citizen of this planet.

Spiritual Attributes

Spiritually, the World is about the law of universality. As you complete spiritual lessons, you allow others to do the same, so that everyone grows and evolves. You are connected to them as they are to you.

Key Words for the World

Oneness, completion, responsibility, actualization

Palmistry Identification

Earth + Fire

In the hands, the World archetype is represented by two elements which can appear in the hands in two ways: short fingers, square palm, Earth, with numerous, sharp, thick lines, or short fingers, rectangular palm, Fire, with just a few deep lines. Here are hand print examples of the World archetype:

The World Hand Print Example 1

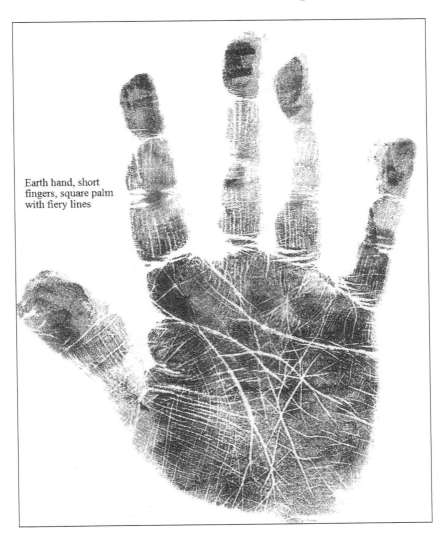

Earth hand, short
fingers, square palm
with fiery lines

The World Hand Print Example 2

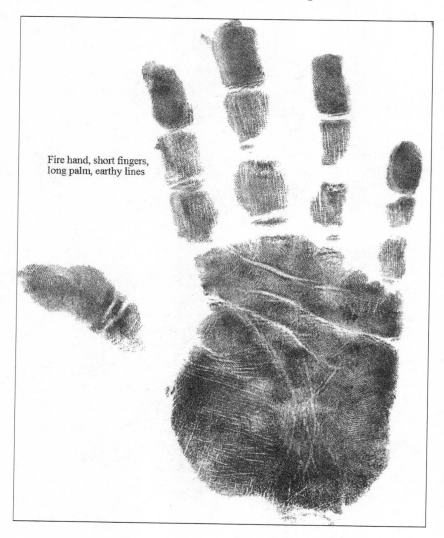

Fire hand, short fingers,
long palm, earthy lines

Examples and Exercises

Mudra

To connect to the World archetype in a mudra, place all fingertips to each other, index to index, middle to middle and so on, with the fingers spread gently apart in a rounded fashion.

Questions for Growth and Coaches Tips

1. What do I envision for the planet? Look at what you want for everyone. This may be a popular ideal or something more esoteric. Your focus may be on people, animals, environment or the earth itself. What speaks to your heart?
2. What individual steps can I take that are more globally oriented? The answer to this question may be as simple as saying a prayer for the planet, or doing a planetary meditation. Perhaps you have a neighbor from a different country, have you made him feel welcome or alienated?
3. How do I show inner and outer beauty? Recognize where you focus your attention. This is what you are bringing more of into the world.

4. In what global areas do I feel disconnected? Is there some area in your life that is out of alignment with the greater good of the world? For example, are you not re-cycling in an area where it's easy to recycle, or wasting water during a drought?

5. What is my bigger planetary mission? Make a statement of your personal mission, or purpose. Then take that statement and apply it globally. For example, I feel that my purpose is to share my passionate wisdom with oth-ers to empower them in living their authentic destiny. Globally, if everyone were living authentically, the world would be full of peace, joy and love.

Truth Statements for the World

1. I am connected to all things in the universe.
2. I love the earth and being part of this world.
3. I accept my individual responsibility as a member of this planet.
4. I express my inner and outer beauty to inspire others.
5. I know and live my life purpose every day.

Chakra Association

Heart, Crown

Identifying Imbalances

Too much World results in losing the self and your own in-dividuality, sometimes falling into martyrdom. Too little World results in being overly selfish, not caring or realizing how your actions and thoughts affect others or the planet.

The World at Home

At home, the World lives with an awareness of structure, home materials and recycling. She is compassionate toward pets and other family members. Always staying busy, she may enjoy gardening or just putting worldly things around the home that remind her of her travels.

The World at Work

At work, the World is difficult to pin down. She's always on the move and has a tremendous amount of energy. She gets most excited by new projects that benefit everyone. She does well in global nonprofit projects, or with innovations that empower others to live more globally conscious lives. Sitting at a desk is not something she enjoys. She needs to be careful about making others feel lazy or inferior due to her naturally high level of energy. She also needs to be careful about a tendency to be condescending.

The World in Relationships

In relationships, the World archetype enjoys creating a sense of home with her partner, whether she's in the backyard or traveling across the planet. She seeks to bond deeply with a single person so that both may grow into their potential. Since it's hard for her to sit still, she needs a partner who doesn't get exhausted by this type of energy, or allows her the freedom to be independent. It's also better for her to have many other things going on besides the relationship itself, or she will feel stifled and trapped. She appreciates a partner who has the same ideals toward global preservation, since this is such an important part of her belief system.

Best Compatibility

Lovers, Sun, Judgement

Good Compatibility

Magician, High Priestess, Empress, Emperor, Chariot, Tower

Challenging Compatibility

Fool, Hermit, Death, Star, Moon

Opposite Archetype

Star

Famous World Archetypes

Martin Luther King, Jr., Robert Downey, Jr., Russell Wilson

Chapter 22

22–Putting it All Together

"The privilege of a lifetime is being who
you are." – Joseph Campbell

THANK YOU FOR TAKING THIS JOURNEY THROUGH
the pathway of the archetypes. As a quick recap, I'd like to summarize each of the archetypes in its most authentic expression. Remember, even though I refer to an archetype as male or female, anyone may possess any archetype.

The Fool

The Fool is a beautiful, young-at-heart spirit. He may surprise you with his arrival into your life, but it's a welcome arrival because he is fun to be around and knows how to have a good time. He doesn't worry about the future because he knows the future will take care of itself and he will be just fine. His creative energy is full of enthusiasm and joy in the present moment. He looks at life as an adventure, full of infinite possibilities.

The Magician

The Magician is a magical manifestor. He knows he has all the tools he needs to create his desired outcome, even though he doesn't know exactly how it's going to happen. He is full of ideas and is excited to put them into practice, either himself or by delegating to others. He has great enthusiasm for life and is extremely intelligent, clever and a little mischievous. His motto is that it's better to make the attempt than not, even if failure is a possibility.

The High Priestess

The High Priestess is a strong and powerful woman. She uses her deep, intuitive insights to govern and direct her life. She has no need for outside approval to make important decisions. Her inner world drives her outer world. She is calm and serene in her interaction with others and very adaptable to her surroundings. With an unwavering certainty, she goes through life on her own terms, setting an example for others to follow.

The Empress

The Empress loves and values all of life. She exudes nurturing energy through her body and interaction with others. She is a steward for the earth; caring for nature, plants and animals. Everything and everyone around her benefits from her abundant care. She is patient for the harvest, willing to put in the necessary work for her job and family, while enjoying the process along the way. She is equally comfortable being alone, completing tasks of importance to her and her own growth.

The Emperor

The Emperor is a powerful and inspiring man. He creates foundations that are meant to last. He is willing to work hard for his empire and must be in complete charge of it. His capacity for results is astounding and he has more energy than most to do what is necessary to create those results. His vision is expansive and grounding at the same time. He inspires others to do more and be more. He makes an incredible ally, but a fierce enemy.

The Hierophant

The Hierophant is the wise, traditional teacher. Also known as the High Priest, he gathers wisdom from the past to continue the tried-and-true formulas that have worked for generations. His benevolence assists his followers in reaching their own enlightenment and understanding of the world. He is patient, kind and understanding of other people's growth. He understands the challenges that people face and sets the example for people to follow.

The Lovers

The Lovers is a challenging archetype to own. Being balanced in feminine and masculine qualities requires development in reasoning combined with emotion and spirituality. He or she is comfortable integrating these qualities through activities and relationships. Full of life and passion, the Lovers personifies sensuality in his or her entire being.

The Chariot

The Chariot sets the example for movement and action. He is balanced in emotional and mental qualities and inspires others through his high ideals. Having found his vehicle, he charges through life with enthusiasm and energy that few can match. He likes to be in charge and show others the way.

Strength

Strength does not force her will onto others to achieve her aims. Rather, she practices loving kindness to display her power. Always looking to learn more about herself and the world around her, Strength holds a bigger vision for a better world and what is possible.

The Hermit

The Hermit takes the independent path toward enlightenment. Incredibly curious and intelligent, he is selective with whom he studies and interacts. A quiet strength exudes from him, but other people may not realize how much he knows, since he does not always share his knowledge unless he's asked. When he finds his path, he can be at the top in his field.

The Wheel of Fortune

The Wheel of Fortune is creative and passionate. He knows that luck is something you create, not something that happens to you. He has a magnetic personality, and others find him reasonable and fun to be around. He is at his best with a variety of creative projects appreciated by other people. He enjoys the spotlight and being the center of attention.

Justice

Justice looks for fairness in all areas of her life. She is balanced and impartial, making a wonderful mediator, listener and counselor. She balances work and play, creating harmony in her own life. She spends an appropriate amount of time by herself and with others, inspiring people around her to find balance within themselves.

The Hanged Man

An integration of opposing elements, action and stillness are created to gain a new perspective. The Hanged Man is willing to give up part of himself in exchange for something better. Another challenging archetype, he succeeds when he's comfortable with himself, regardless of other people's opinions or lack of understanding. Being a natural pot stirrer, he shakes up the status quo and allows for innovation and new ways of being to emerge.

Death

Death sets a wonderful example through shedding and eliminating whatever is complete. He understands that from every ending there is a new beginning, a transformation to higher and higher possibilities. He inspires others to let go and begin again.

Temperance

Temperance shows others what is working through the middle road by staying away from extreme thinking and behavior. He sets the perfect example of how to be reasonable and inspired through his creative solutions and high ideals. Temperance is easy to get along with and makes a wonderful, caring friend.

The Devil

The Devil is a clever, fun-loving person. He uses humor to assist others in overcoming their fears. Infinitely curious, the Devil seeks to know what bondages exist in the human psyche so they may be freed. At his best, he is aware of not only external or superficial beauty, but also inner beauty and the playfulness that exists in everyone.

The Tower

The Tower is a very strong, powerful archetype. If you're not ready for him, he may come across as overly blunt, striking the truth to awaken you to a new reality. His motives are pure and he seeks enlightenment for everyone, shining the truth and purging outdated systems and beliefs. If he comes across your path, don't be afraid. Listen to his insights as opportunities for growth and advancement, even if they call for some destruction in your life. He can help you embrace change.

The Star

The Star is a gentle archetype, helping you realize your dreams and aspirations. Willing to develop her own talents, she also supports you in seeing and growing your own. Everyone deserves to live their dreams. Let the Star assist you in realizing this truth. She may come across as a dreamer, but her thought-fulness and emotional balance set the stage for unfolding our natural gifts.

The Moon

Another challenging archetype, the Moon understands the cycles and phases of life. She takes time to retreat into her deep, intuitive self and reflect on the cycle she's in and the cycle emerging. She keeps part of herself hidden, not consciously but by virtue of her nature. Getting to know her well may take some time, but it's worth the effort. She can help others uncover their hidden secrets and heal.

The Sun

The Sun is outgoing and luminous. He is completely aware of his talents and takes full responsibility in developing them and sharing them with the world. He takes his craft seriously and expects others to do the same. The Sun has more energy than most of the other archetypes, so he may find others having a hard time keeping up with him.

Judgement

Judgement combines thinking with personal responsibility to transform. He holds the truth mirror for your own ability to release limiting thoughts and claim your power in your purpose. He understands the proper time and space for things to emerge, not rushing them or slowing them down. This archetype, liked the Hanged Man, is an integration of opposing elements.

The World

The last archetype, the World, expresses responsibility in the larger context. She understands that we are all one, we are all connected. She feels most complete when working toward a greater goal that helps everyone. She inspires others by setting an example through her larger connection.

Conclusion

Now that you are familiar with all of the archetypes, it is my hope and wish that you use this book as a daily tool to connect with your own subconscious influences and live a more authentic life. Getting to know your own archetypes can be very powerful and enlightening. They can become your inner masterminds, guiding your everyday actions and decisions. Discovering other peoples' archetypes helps you understand those around you and why they behave in certain ways that may be completely different from your own. No one archetype is more knowing or correct; each one simply demonstrates our individual uniqueness and motivation.

If you have two or three archetypes, you may be wondering which one is dominant. The answer to that is none of them, but you may recognize one archetype as more dominant in one area of your life and another in a separate area. For example, let's say you have two archetypes, the Empress and the Moon. At work, you may be more aware of the Empress, especially if you're in a growth cycle or you just got promoted. While at home, you may feel more in touch with the Moon, withdrawing into a spiritual practice to understand yourself better. Or you may find that one has been more central during a certain stage of your life. As you become more aware of them, you will probably find all of your archetypes layering over and through each other, like a tapestry. Empower yourself in new ways by recognizing your own imbalances and invoking your archetypes to strengthen and guide yourself more authentically.

I've debated whether or not to share my own archetypes with you. I decided that it might be fun for you to get to know me better as your guide through this journey, but I specifically chose to wait until now since I didn't want to bias any of the archetypes. My three archetypes are the Lovers, the Chariot and the Hanged Man. I hope you recognize all three of these in the preceding pages – a balance of energetic and soft discourse, a vehicle for sharing stories, and a new perspective on yourself, palmistry and tarot.

I encourage you to look at the hands of the people you know and get to know their archetypes as well. It can be so enlightening! I firmly believe that understanding each other inspires greater compassion by changing our perspective through a sense of wonder and discovery.

I also find it extremely useful to use the exercises from each of the chapters to develop yourself more fully and broaden your abilities to grow and expand. I encourage you to buy a deck of tarot cards, or any set of cards that include the Major Arcana, and pull a daily archetype card. Whether you pull your archetype or not, the card has power to assist you in your daily life and show you something new. Keep a journal and meditate on your questions; you may be surprised at what comes up for you. Personally, I like to journal in the morning right after meditating, when the day is still fresh and it sets me up to be more mindful. Or, as you set your own intentions and affirmations, think about which archetype would be the most helpful to invoke and place your hands in the corresponding mudra. I used a variety of mudras recently with a list of my own goals, and felt myself align more powerfully with each one. I could feel the emotion behind the intention so much more quickly and efficiently. If you're not sure which archetype belongs with which goal, just draw a card for guidance. Play with the material and have some fun with it. Please share your stories and epiphanies on the World of Hands Facebook page.

I wish you peace, love and joy as you learn more about the stories in your own hands and how to live your own authentic destiny.

Appendix 1

Cynthia has created her own Palmistry Inspiration Cards that correspond with the markings in your hands. While not a traditional tarot deck, this deck can be used with the archetypes as a divination tool and pathway into deeper understanding of palmistry. Below is a list of the palmistry card equivalent to the tarot Major Arcana. If you are interested in ordering your own deck of Palmistry Inspiration Cards, they are available through www.palmistrycards.com.

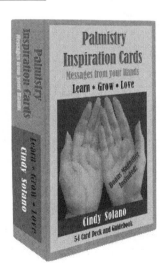

Tarot Card	**Palmistry Inspiration Card**
Fool	Mercury Challenge
Magician	Thumb
High Priestess	Loop of Intuition
Empress	Venus
Emperor	Zone of Organization
Hierophant	Saturn
Lovers	Zone of Sensuality
Chariot	Zone of Ambition
Strength	Ring of Solomon
Hermit	Cave Line
Wheel of Fortune	Loop of Humor
Justice	Ego Loop
Hanged Man	Excitement Lines
Death	Traveler's Fork
Temperance	Aspiration Lines
Devil	Girdles of Venus
Tower	Healing Stigmata
Star	Star of Apollo
Moon	Luna
Sun	Apollo
Judgement	Fate Line
World	Saturn Challenge

Appendix 2

This appendix is for your use as a quick reference to identify imbalances in actions, emotions or chakras in terms of which archetypes they relate to. After matching imbalances to archetypes below, you may then refer back to the chapters for those archetypes and use the exercises listed for balance. If there is more than one archetype listed for an imbalance, go to your personal archetype first if it's in the list. For example, if you are suffering from anxiety, this could be an imbalance with the Fool, Wheel of Fortune or Temperance. If your hand shape corresponds with Temperance (Air hand, long Apollo finger), refer to that chapter first.

__Action Imbalance__	__Archetype Association__
Addictions	Devil, Fool, Tower, Moon
Bad luck	Wheel of Fortune, Magician, Chariot, Judgement
Betrayal	Strength, Judgement
Burning others	Sun, Emperor, Strength, Justice
Clinging	Death, Empress, Chariot, Temperance
Coldness	High Priestess, Empress, Lovers, Hermit, Sun
Consequences, Not learning from	Judgement, Hierophant, Hermit, Hanged Man

Cycles, out of sync	Moon, Judgement
Dark Night of the Soul	Death, Devil, Tower
Debauchery	Devil, Tower
Denial	Fool, Hanged Man, Devil, Moon
Dictator	Emperor, Strength, Justice
Dogmatic	Hierophant
Dominating	Strength, Emperor
External Only Focus	Hermit, High Priestess, Devil, World
Failure	Magician, Emperor, Chariot, Sun, World
Fixed perspective	Hanged Man, Hierophant
Foolish choices	Fool, Hierophant, Hermit, Wheel of Fortune, Star
Greedy	Wheel of Fortune, Emperor, Chariot, Strength, Justice
Hoarding	Tower
Ignorant	Hermit, High Priestess, Fool, Hierophant, Moon
Incompletion	Moon, Chariot, Death, Tower, Star, World
Indecisive	Temperance, Magician, Star, Chariot
Judgmental	Justice, Judgement, Hierophant, Emperor, Hanged Man
Keeping wisdom to self	High Priestess, Hierophant, Star
Know-it-All	Hermit, High Priestess, Hierophant, Emperor, Judgement, World, Justice
Loss of Self	World, Strength, Death, Devil, Star, Tower
Love Unreceived	Empress, Lovers, World

Lunacy	Moon, Fool, High Priestess
Manipulation	Magician, Emperor, Strength, Justice, Judgement
Martyrdom	World
Micromanaging	Wheel of Fortune, Chariot, Emperor, Strength, Magician
Over-mothering	Empress
Patterns Repeating	Wheel of Fortune, Moon, Judgement
Procrastination	Chariot, Hanged Man, Death, Tower, Moon, Star, Hermit
Prostitute	Lovers, Fool, Justice, Death, Devil
Rebel	Hanged Man, Magician, Hierophant, Hermit, Temperance, Devil
Restructure challenge	Tower, Death, Emperor, Hierophant, Chariot
Rigid	Temperance, Hanged Man, Judgement, Emperor
Selfish	World, Magician, Empress, Emperor, Lovers, Hermit
Smothering	Empress, Emperor, Lovers, Strength, Judgement, World
Stagnation	Tower, Death, Judgement
Starvation	Devil, Fool, Hanged Man, Moon
Talents known but undeveloped	Star, Hermit, High Priestess
Talents unknown	Star, Hermit, Hierophant, Magician
Time/space incompatibilities	Judgement, Wheel of Fortune

Tunnel Vision	Chariot, Hanged Man, Emperor, Justice, World, Hierophant
Victim	Fool, Wheel of Fortune
Vigilante	Justice, Hanged Man
Virginal	Lovers, High Priestess, Hermit, Hierophant
Weak and ineffective	Strength, Magician, World
Weak Foundation	Emperor, Fool, Devil, Star

Emotional Imbalance	**Archetype Association**
Abandonment	Lovers, World
Anger	Emperor, Chariot, Justice, Tower, Sun, Judgemen
Anxious/Worried	Fool, Wheel of Fortune, Temperance
Bitter	Justice, Fool, Wheel of Fortune, World
Confusion	High Priestess, Hierophant, Hermit, Hanged Man, Moon
Depression	Fool, Sun
Discouraged	Chariot, Wheel of Fortune, Star, Judgement
Fear	Fool, Devil, Moon
Guilt	Hierophant, Lovers, Wheel of Fortune, Justice, Devil, Judgement, World
Helpless	Magician, Emperor, Chariot, Strength, Justice, Hanged Man
Jealous	Emperor, Lovers, Chariot, Devil, Star

Lost	High Priestess, Hierophant, Hermit, Death, Tower
Overwhelm	Tower, Sun
Pessimism	Wheel of Fortune, Sun
Resentment	Empress, Hermit, Hanged Man, Death, Moon
Scarcity	Empress, Wheel of Fortune, Magician, Sun
Scattered	Magician, Fool, Moon, Tower
Self Worth Issues	Strength, Devil, Tower, Star, Sun, Judgement
Seriousness	Fool, High Priestess, Hierophant, Justice, Death, Devil, Tower, Sun
Uncaring	High Priestess, World, Empress, Justice, Judgement
Uncompromising	Temperance, Emperor, Strength, Chariot, Wheel of Fortune
Unforgiving	Justice, Judgement
Withdrawn	High Priestess, Hermit, Moon

Chakra Imbalance	**Archetype Association**
Root (1st) Chakra	Fool, Emperor, Hermit, Devil
Sacral (2nd) Chakra	Empress, Lovers, Temperance, Star, Moon
Solar Plexus (3rd) Chakra	Magician, Emperor, Chariot, Hanged Man, Star, Sun
Heart (4th) Chakra	Empress, Lovers, Strength, Temperance, Sun, World
Throat (5th) Chakra	Hierophant, Justice, Devil, Sun, Judgement
Third Eye (6th) Chakra	High Priestess, Hierophant, Strength, Hermit, Hanged Man, Tower, Judgement
Crown (7th) Chakra	Magician, Wheel of Fortune, Death, Tower, World

Appendix 3

This appendix is a quick reference of the palmistry identification for each of the archetypes.

Element & Finger Combinations	Archetype
Air + Jupiter	Strength
Air + Saturn	Hierophant
Air + Apollo	Temperance
Air + Mercury	Devil
Earth + Jupiter	Emperor
Earth + Saturn	Empress
Earth + Apollo	Sun
Earth + Mercury	Hermit
Fire + Jupiter	Chariot
Fire + Saturn	Lovers
Fire + Apollo	Wheel of Fortune
Fire + Mercury	Magician
Water + Jupiter	Death
Water + Saturn	Justice
Water + Apollo	Fool
Water + Mercury	High Priestess

Double Element Combinations

Air + Earth	Judgement
Air + Fire	Tower
Air + Water	Star
Earth + Fire	World
Earth + Water	Moon
Fire + Water	Hanged Man

About the Author

Photo by Cathy Schraiban

Cynthia Clark is a hand analyst expert, intuitive life coach, healer, author and teacher. She offers hand analysis training, readings, coaching, workshops and other empowerment products. You may learn more about them by visiting www. WorldofHands.com or www.Cynthia-Clark.com.

An Invitation For You

Cynthia would love to stay in touch with you! Sign up for a free Life Purpose Assessment at www.WorldofHands.com and receive updates and information from Cynthia through her newsletter. Join her Authentic Destiny Online Coaching Program and be part of a larger community of like-minded people.

Want to take your learning about the archetypes to the next level? Cynthia offers expanded training and meditations to help you connect and deepen your experience. You may also share your own stories. Please go to www.storiesinyour-hands.com.